EXPERIENCES

OF AN

ARMY SURGEON IN INDIA

EXPERIENCES

OF AN

ARMY SURGEON IN INDIA.

BY

C. A. GORDON, M. D., C.B.

GYAN

Published by

Gyan Publishing House
5, Ansari Road
Daryaganj, New Delhi-110002
Phone: 011-47034999, 9811692060
E-mail: books@gyanbooks.com

Distribution Network
gyanbooks.com
India, USA, Canada, UK, Australia

ISBN: 978-81-212-8402-8 (HB)
First Published, 1872

2nd Impression 2024

Printed at: Gyan Press, Delhi.

EXPERIENCES OF AN ARMY SURGEON IN INDIA
Author: C. A. GORDON

EXPERIENCES

OF

AN ARMY SURGEON IN INDIA.

EXPERIENCES

OF AN

ARMY SURGEON IN INDIA.

BY

C. A. GORDON, M.D. C.B.,

DEPUTY INSPECTOR-GENERAL OF HOSPITALS.

Reprinted from the MEDICAL PRESS AND CIRCULAR.

LONDON:

BAILLIERE, TINDALL, AND COX,
20 KING WILLIAM STREET, STRAND.

1872.

TABLE OF CONTENTS.

EXPERIENCES

OF A

REGIMENTAL SURGEON IN INDIA.

WOUNDS AND INJURIES.

WOUNDS and external injuries are generally believed to constitute the especial province of the military surgeon. That soldiers are, from the nature of their life and the casualties in campaigns, more liable to injuries from external violence than persons in civil life appears self-evident, but that the proportion of deaths from this cause is not excessive when compared with that from the ordinary diseases incidental to a hot climate will be best illustrated by the table on the following page.

The numbers of men and officers who have, on the various occasions when the 10th Regiment, in which I had the honour to serve, was engaged in action, been killed on the field are, as a matter of course, not included among the above. They will be more particularly alluded to in their proper place; but, for the sake of indicating side by side the rates of admissions and deaths from external injuries compared with but a small portion of

C

	Wounds and Accidents.	Soldiers. Strength, 11,780.				Officers. Strength, 409.			
		Cases Ad-mitted.	Died.	Deaths per 100 Admitted	Cases per 100 Strength.	Cases Ad-mitted.	Died.	Deaths per 100 Admitted	Cases per 100 Strength.
1	Vulnus Sclopitorum ...	254	20	7·87	2·15	4	1	25	0·97
2	Vulnus Incisum	109	...	...	0·92	4	...	...	0·97
3	Amputatio	17	2	11·76	0·14	...	...	...	...
4	Fractura	22	...	...	0·18	4	...	...	0·97
5	Luxatio	6	...	...	0·05	2	...	...	0·48
6	Subluxatio	128	...	...	1·08	15	...	...	3·36
7	Contusio	338	...	...	2·86	34	...	...	8·29
8	Ambustio	23	...	...	0·19	1	...	...	0·24
9	Concussio Cerebri	1	...	...	...	...	...	...	...
	Total	898	22	...	...	64	1	...	...

diseases incidental to Europeans resident in India, let us briefly enumerate a few of the latter :—

Diseases.	Soldiers.		Officers.	
	Total Admitted.	Died per cent. Treated.	Total Admitted.	Died per cent. Treated.
Pulmonic	1050	6·90	55	,,
Fevers	6273	2·88	283	1·41
Stomach and Bowels	3043	8·21	144	2·77
Liver and Spleen	871	6·19	29	10·34
Brain and Nerves	322	17·39	16	18·75
Wounds and Accidents	898	2·44	64	1·56

These figures show that external injuries do not by any means constitute so important a class of cases in India as might probably be supposed, and that, with the exception of the now happily rare occasions when our troops are called upon to take the field, surgery must be considered as holding in military practice a very secondary place to medicine.

Before entering upon the consideration of the statistics of the particular injuries, I would observe that there are some whose very absence must attract attention. Of these are punctured wounds, such as are caused by a bayonet thrust, and the various descriptions of poisoned wounds.

The rarity of bayonet wounds in hospital is a general subject of remark by military surgeons in India, and must arise from one of two causes: either that the enemy does not often allow our white troops to come to hand-to-hand conflict with them, or else that the wounds inflicted by a bayonet are so generally fatal that the person injured dies on the field. The latter explanation is, I suspect, the true one, for in the battles that during the fifteen years, from 1842 to 1857, have taken place between our forces and Mahrattas, Scindians, and Sikhs, there are numerous instances of our soldiers, when entering the enemies' batteries or storming fortresses, encountering the most desperate and deadly opposition. Under such circumstances the musket is comparatively little used, the bayonet being almost alone trusted to by the English, as the same weapon and heavy sword, or tulwar, have unquestionably been by those races.

With the exception of one of hydrophobia not another case attributable to poisoned wound is recorded. This is the more remarkable when we consider the abundance of venomous reptiles and insects that occur in India, and that soldiers are so constantly unavoidably, or by their own want of care, exposed to danger from such sources. Although snake bites are comparatively rare among white troops, there is no doubt that many cases among all classes of persons in the regiment occurred, where injuries were inflicted, by the smaller class of such creatures as scorpions, centipedes, spiders, wasps, and mosquitoes, while I have myself seen vesication, attended by much pain and heat of the part, occur from a common wall lizard falling upon the uncovered skin of a person, as described by Hasselquist.*

On the 10th February, 1846, the 10th Regiment, consisting of 742 men and 34 officers, was present in the action of Sobraon. Of the men 29 were killed on the field, or a proportion of 3·87 per cent., 136 men were wounded, or 18·32 per cent., making the proportion of casualties among them 22·19 per cent.; of the officers 1 was killed, or a proportion of 2·94 per cent., and 2 wounded, being a ratio of 5·88, thus making the casualties among them 8·22, or 13·37 per cent. less than what occurred among the soldiers.

Among the affairs in which the regiment took part during the second Sikh campaign, was that of the 9th September, 1848, when a night attack was made with four companies upon one of the enemies' fortified out-

---

* Ptyodactylus Gecko.

posts at Mooltan. This attack is stated to have, for the time, been unsuccessful, and we learn that of the men engaged 9 were killed and 33 wounded; 1 officer being severely wounded. The precise strength of this detachment does not appear, but it is fair to presume that the companies were made up to their full strength for the occasion, in which case there would have been 400 men and 13 officers.

According to these we should find the ratio

	Of Killed.	Of Wounded.	Of Casualties.
Among Men	2·25	8·25	10·50
Among Officers...	,,	7·69	7·69

Here, again, we find the ratio of casualties in battle to be less among the officers than the men.

The assault was renewed shortly after day-light on the 12th September. Six companies of the regiment formed part of the attacking column, and, according to the report of the medical officer in charge at the time, "although hundreds of the enemy were slain, we yet had to lament the fall of many gallant and brave soldiers." Our loss consisted of 1 officer killed and 2 wounded, 5 rank and file killed and 29 wounded, so that if, as before, we suppose the companies complete, we shall have 600 men and 19 officers going into this action.

This would give us a ratio

	Of Killed.	Of Wounded.	Of Casualties.
Among Men	0·83	4·83	5·66
Among Officers...	5.26	10·53	15·79

Here we have the ratio of casualties among the officers nearly three times the amount among men.

At the battle of Goojerat, fought on the 21st February, 1849, the regiment had 7 men killed and 52 wounded, but the officers do not appear to have suffered at all on this occasion. We have reason to suppose that the regiment went into action at Goojerat 700 strong in men, so that, according to this, the ratio would be

	Of Killed.	Of Wounded.	Of Casualties.
Among Men	1	7·42	8·42

With regard to the precise nature of the wounds of men admitted into the field hospital during those operations we find the following to be an abstract; namely—

Stump cases	9
Injuries of the head	2
" " neck	2
" " thorax	3
" " abdomen	3
Compound fractures	2
Injuries to joints	3
Wounds of soft parts	22
Simple and miscellaneous wounds . .	10
Incised wounds	7
Burns	1—64

That tetanus occasionally occurs among soldiers in India who are wounded is well known, but that the affection is not so frequent as many persons believe appears in the fact that no case of it happened in any of the cases to which the above figures refer, neither did hospital gangrene show itself.

The surgeon remarks, in alluding to the absence of hospital gangrene, that he attributes this *to the great attention paid to cleanliness.* He also observes that during the campaign (Second Sikh War) the general health of the men was good, and this was in a great measure attributable to the attention that was paid to the clothing of the men, and to the adoption of flooring of wood in their tents while in a standing camp, by which the beds were kept raised from the cold ground. Here, then, we have the explanation of the general efficiency of soldiers in India on a campaign, the small percentage of sickness among them, and the favourable and rapid recovery of those who are wounded otherwise than very severely. These circumstances are in themselves so important that I recapitulate them :—

1st. Cleanliness.
2nd. Good clothing.
3rd. Elevation of beds from the cold ground.

We have in India two other valuable adjuucts for maintaining the health and efficiency of the men; namely, regular and well-cooked meals, prepared by people maintained for that particular purpose, and good and ample protection in the superior description of tents supplied by the local government to regiments; nor must I omit to observe that, during ordinary marches, an ample supply of straw is always available to be placed under the rugs on which the men in health sleep.

The cases of gunshot wounds do not seem to have constituted one half the entire number of casualties that occurred among the soldiers at the battle of Sobraon, 55 men suffering from injuries of this description having been admitted out of a total of 136. Of these 55, six died shortly after being admitted, exclusive of those who underwent amputation.

At the affairs of 9th and 12th September, 1848, already mentioned, the gunshot and incised wounds were in more equal proportions, and at Goojerat the wounds were almost entirely caused by gunshot. The nature of the military tactics employed during an action influences the character of the injuries, inseparable from the engagement of an infantry regiment with the enemy. Thus at Sobraon, where the regiment was called upon to make a rapid advance and carry batteries, the celerity with which they charged the Sikh guns diminished the degree to which the men would otherwise have suffered from a heavy fire of artillery; but, in the hand-to-hand conflict in which they immediately became engaged while wresting the guns from their artillery, the wounds were almost all inflicted by swords.

In the night attack made on an outpost at Mooltan, on the 9th September, when our men were exposed to a heavy fire from walls, the mass of casualties consisted of musket and "zambouruk," or swivel gunshot wounds.

On the 12th of the same month, when they captured the post, they had the same large proportion of wounds from fire-arms, prior to an entrance being effected; but after that, when they came to hand-to-hand conflict with the defenders, the injuries, as before, were from the "tulwars," or native sword.

At the battle of Goojerat, which, as is well known, was almost entirely decided by artillery, the nature of the wounds was all occasioned by grape and round shot.

If we draw our conclusions solely from the numerical return, we should be inclined to consider that because no death appears by it to have occurred from incised wounds, injuries of this description are, therefore, of inconsiderable danger. Actual experience, however, must convince us that they are far otherwise, for, while many cases of gunshot wounds, of an evidently mortal nature, are brought to hospital, and thus included in the hospital returns, an incised wound of such a nature as to be mortal, usually terminates existence almost instantaneously, so that the majority that come under notice are mere cuts of the soft parts; sometimes of fearful extent, no doubt, and frequently inplicating other tissues, but, nevertheless, in their nature comparatively free from actual danger to life. The vast majority of cases of this description healed without the occurrence of any untoward symptoms, and their treatment appears, as a general rule, to have been very simple.

The statistics regarding amputation are, it must be allowed, very incomplete; it is evident, however, that the majority of cases here recorded were instances of disease. It, moreover, would appear that in the hurry unavoidable in battle, some cases of amputation were not distinguished from the gunshot wound that rendered the operation necessary.

We learn that among five patients, four of whom underwent primary amputation, three died. The one subjected to secondary amputation recovered ; but this is manifestly too small a number to be brought forward for or against either of those measures.

Fractures and dislocations are by no means so frequent, apparently, among infantry soldiers in India as might be supposed. They occur under the same circumstances as in Britain ; but there are some points with reference to fractures that deserve notice. When a person sustains an accident of this nature during the cold season, his general health being at the time unimpaired, and he so situated that he can be treated in his own regimental hospital, the progress of such cases is much the same, and his chances of a good recovery similar to what they would be in the United Kingdom. If, on the other hand, the regiment is on a march, and the person has to be carried in a dooley a distance of ten to fifteen miles daily, it is clear that with the apparatus necessarily applied in such circumstances, there is not the same chance of good and straight union taking place that there would be under more favourable auspices. And again, when a person already debilitated by fever, or other endemic disease, meets with a fracture in India during the hot season, not only is he likely to suffer severely from sympathetic fever, and thus have his powers still more debilitated, but there may be insufficient action to carry on the process of reparation. Callus may not be thrown out at all, or if secreted in the first instance, may cease before it is sufficiently consolidated, and thus the solution in the bone remains unrepaired.

Sprains and bruises appear, as a rule, to be of less frequent occurrence among soldiers in India than in the United Kingdom; nor is this to be wondered at when we bear in mind how little inducement there is in India for the men to wander far from their barracks—they cannot mix with the residents as they do at home—and when indulging in their cups and quarrelsome, the violence they sometimes offer to the Asiatic is not quite so certain of being returned as it would be by the lower orders of most garrison towns in Britain.

The men of the 10th Regiment were fortunate in escaping severe burns in action by the explosion of mines, tumbrils, &c.; but other corps have not been equally so, and when such injuries happen they constitute some of the most painful and terrible that have to be treated. The slighter kinds are often occasioned by trifling with gunpowder, or by the unexpected explosion of a musket; but, from the general want of fires in barracks in India, this class of accident is less common than they are in the United Kingdom.

It is now a tolerably well established fact that the destruction of one-third of the cuticular surface is sufficient to render death inevitable, and that cases of burn usually terminate fatally in consequence of the occurrence of exhausting diarrhœa.

The last accident recorded is concussion of the brain. It must be a matter of surprise how casualties of this description are so few as they are among bodies of troops in India. In fact, this very rarity is more deserving of remark than their occurrence, and this circumstance tends to show still more clearly the correctness of the remark already made—namely, that external injuries in India, even including those inseparable from engagements with the enemy, are a source of inconsiderable loss to a regiment when compared to the climatorial diseases to which it is constantly exposed during its service in that country.

The reader need hardly be informed that in 1857 the

Sepoy mutiny occurred. The regiment to which these notes specially refer had the misfortune, in July of that year, to sustain a heavy loss in officers and men, by a part of it falling into an ambuscade at Arrah, on which occasion, of six officers one was killed on the field, and two wounded, of whom one shortly afterwards died; of 152 men, there were killed on the spot 47, and wounded, more or less severely, 32. Thus there occurred on this single occasion a far greater loss of life than the corps had sustained during some of the hard fought battles in which it had taken a part previous to the subjugation of the Punjaub being completed.

Throughout the other affairs in which the regiment was engaged during that year, 2 officers were wounded, 7 men killed, and 43 wounded more or less severely. Thus we learn that, in an average of 705 men, the ratio for the whole period was of killed before the enemy 7·65 of strength. Of the 75 wounded, there died 7, or 2·42 more; that is, 10·07 men out of every 100 were killed or died of their wounds during the year. The deaths from all other causes at, and absent from, head-quarters were 59, or at the rate of 8·36 per cent. strength in addition; or a grand total of 18·43 per 100. But great as is the list of casualties here given, it by no means represents the entire loss sustained by the regiment during this eventful year; 44 men were, by the nature of their wounds, or other circumstances incidental to service, incapacitated for continuing at their duty, and as a result had to be invalided and sent to England.

To render this fearful state of casualties still more evident, I remark that, in an average strength for the year of 705, there were—

Killed in an ambuscade . . .	47
Killed at head-quarters during the Lucknow campaign	7
Of 75 wounded, there died . . .	17
Died of disease at, and absent from, head-quarters during the year	59
Invalided and sent to England .	44
Total casualtics	174

Showing a rate of decrease, from all these causes, of 24·68 per 100 strength per annum !

The following table shows the nature of the wounds and injuries from which our soldiers suffered ; those injuries that did not prove fatal on the spot being alone enumerated namely :—

	Injury.	Occurred.	Died.	Invalided.
1	Vulnus Sclopitorum ...	60	10 [1]	11
2	„ Incisum.........	8	0	0
3	„ Punctatum.....	1	0	0
4	Amputatio..............	5	1	0
5	Fractura...............	1	0	0
6	Subluxatio	7	0	0
7	Contusio...............	13	0	0
8	Ambustio	6	6	0
9	Concussio Cerebri.......	1	0	1
	Totals...	102	17	12

1 Two of these died of Tetanus.

The military surgeon will have no difficulty in gathering from the above figures the nature of the service in which the subjects of the injuries were engaged ; thus the inconsiderable proportion of sword cuts as compared to gunshot wounds indicate as clearly as need be, that our troops were seldom enabled to come to hand-to-hand combat with the rebels ; the almost entire absence of bayonet wounds, there being only one enumerated, and it of very trifling nature, clearly showing that it was no part of the Sepoy's tactics to stand a charge by our indomitable Infantry.

Burns from explosions constitute some of the characteristic injuries that attend a siege ; mines, tumbrels, and expense magazines on such occasions, often explode either by intention or by accident, inflicting the most terrific injuries upon the unfortunate men in the vicinity that it is the lot of the regimental medical officer to witness, among all the terrible sights to which on a campaign he must become accustomed.

What do we learn from the rate of occurrence and mortality of gunshot wounds? Let us first compare what has taken place during the first year of the Indian mutiny, with what happened during two previous campaigns in that country in which the 10th Regiment took a distinguished part.

	Number occurred.	Number died.	Rate of death per 100 treated.
1st year of Sepoy Mutiny ...	60	10	16·66
1st Sikh War ...	55	6	10·81
2nd Sikh War ...	149	14	9·46

We see from these simple figures that on the present occasion the wounds inflicted upon our men have been much more severe in their nature than on either of the two former. How is this? It clearly shows that whereas on these two occasions, the career of the regiment against the enemy was one continued glorious success, the latter being pressed so closely and effectually as to prevent them from taking steady aim, a party of our men on the present occasion were led into a trap where the enemy had it in their power to take deadly aim at their victims, themselves being the while secure from danger. Can anything, therefore, more clearly prove than they do that not only saving of life on the field, but great saving in the severity of wounds that do not prove immediately fatal, are best secured by pressing on rapidly to close quarters with the foe?

The meaning conveyed to the mind by the word "gunshot wound" is, to most people, sufficiently plain, yet if we are asked to define what an injury of this nature really consists of, we have some difficulty in clearly expressing ourselves regarding it. Let me see then what some of our standard authorities say on the subject. Hennen (p. 32) says "that a gunshot injury is a violent contusion with or without solution of continuity, suddenly and rapidly effected by a solid body projected from fire-arms." Druit* is less correct. He states that "they consist of severe contusions with or without solution of continuity," a definition equally applicable to injuries inflicted by a bludgeon in an Irish faction fight as to a wound inflicted by fire-arms. Guthrie† seems to be satisfied with stating generally "that a wound made by a musket-ball is strictly a contused wound." Ballingall does not stop to ask the question what is a gunshot wound.

The ordinary kinds of what are called gun-shot wounds met with on active service are 1st, from cannon-balls, 2nd from fragments of shells, 3rd, from grape, canister, or shrapnell, 4th, from musket bullets, and 5th, from pistol bullets. An injury from a cannon ball must always be severe in its nature, and dangerous in its results. In the early part of its progress a missile of this description ploughs a lane through an advancing column, mangling the unhappy men whom it happens to strike in a manner terrible to look at. After it has expended its force, however, it will often impinge against a person so slightly as not to break the continuity of the skin, perhaps merely inflicting a bruise, but more generally breaking the bones, or if it strike the chest or stomach producing instantaneous death. Cases of this description used to be referred to the wind of the shot. Hennen in his work on "Military Surgery," expresses his belief in such a cause, and at page 94, thus expresses himself, "I should be very far from denying altogether the influence of *the shock*, whether that is electrical or not, because we frequently meet with cases where no local injury can be detected after death. That the compressed air alone or the friction of the ball has no such effect, appears to me satisfactorily proved by the usual arguments drawn from instances of near comrades being killed, or parts of the body being torn off without the individual being destroyed ; and it is rendered if possible still stronger by instances of escape owing to a sudden

* Surgeon's *Vade Mecum.*
† On Gunshot Wounds.

contortion of the body in the attempt of evading the summary military punishment inflicted in some foreign countries by blowing men off from the mouth of a gun.

Among the remarkable cases of injury of this nature, we have that where death has been occasioned by a cannon ball striking a load carried upon the head, *post-mortem* examination failing to detect any lesion of tissue. Sir George Ballingall mentions the case of an officer whose knee-pan was dislocated, as he firmly believes, "by the wind of shot during an action on shipboard," and quotes from Sir Gilbert Blane the instances of two men who were killed in Lord Rodney's action in the West Indies, by balls passing across the pit of the stomach. There is no doubt, however, that in all these cases, actual mechanical contact took place; and two similar cases came under my own observation, in one of which instantaneous death was the result, in the other, fracture of the clavicle.

A man of the 20th Regiment, during the advance upon the guns of the Oude rebels at Sooltanpore, February 23rd, 1858, dropped dead in the ranks at the instant that two others beside him fell wounded by a round shot. Not an injury could for some time be detected; and the placid expression of the face strikingly illustrated what has so often been remarked in death from bullet wounds. The only unnatural appearance was a considerable degree of lividity of the lips and face generally.

This man's chest was afterwards found to have been completely flattened, the sternum absolutely ground to small fragments, yet not a scratch was evident on the skin. The other instance was that of private John Byrne, who was wounded at Humeerpore on the 19th February, 1858; a six-pound shot in its ricochet struck the left side of the chest, over the upper border of the pectoralis major, just grazing the skin. Considerable swelling occurred at once, there was much tenderness, but apparently no fracture. The patient, a very powerful man, was brought to the rear in a state of great mental agitation, but the pulse remained natural. Cold water was applied, a little stimulant given, and by the 21st he suffered only from stiffness and inability to use the left arm. Several days after receiving the injury, on turning himself suddenly in bed he felt a sharp snap, and a transverse fracture of the clavicle was found to have occurred at its middle. The ordinary apparatus for the treatment of that accident was applied. He was sent to the field hospital, when favourable recovery took place. He subsequently rejoined the regiment, and was killed while charging the rebel Sepoys.

Guthrie in his work on "Gunshot Wounds," states that injuries of this description were formerly attributed to the wind of ball, but the opinion was abandoned from a total want of any positive evidence in support of it, whilst much positive evidence could be brought against it. The Baron Larrey explains that a cannon ball is propelled at first with a rectilinear movement, and if, during this part of its course, it strikes against any part of the human body it carries it away, but the ball after having traversed a certain distance, undergoes some change of motion in consequence of the resistance of the atmosphere and the attraction of the earth, and turns on its own axis in addition to the direct impulse received from the explosion of powder. If it should strike any part of the body when the velocity with which the ball is passing is greatly diminished, it does not carry away as in the preceding case, but in consequence of its curvilinear or rolling motion it turns round the part in the same manner as a wheel passes over a limb instead of forcing a passage through it. The soft elastic parts, such as the skin and cellular membrane yield, whilst the bones, muscles, tendons, arteries, &c., offering a greater degree of resistance, are either bruised or fractured. If the ball should strike one of the cavities of the body the viscera suffer in like manner. So far as my experience enables me to form an opinion, I am inclined to believe that this explanation is the correct one. Most extensive swelling and ecchymosis follow injuries of this nature, and the liability of the part injured to suppuration or sphacelus is well known to military surgeons.

Shells are even more destructive to life than cannon balls, for while the latter when they strike only carry death in one direct line, a shell, by virtue of its very nature, sends death and destruction equally on all sides. Besides this, a cannon ball * if discharged a distance of 800 to 1,000 yards leaves sufficient time, before it travels over that distance, to enable men against whom it is directed to take advantage of any means of shelter that may be available. This I have personally witnessed at Lucknow, and there are still officers in the 10th Foot who were present when two companies of that regiment had for several hours a continued duel with one of the rebels' batteries, the fire from which they "kept down," so as to be comparatively harmless.

The histories of all military expeditions teem with illustrations of the effect of active service in enabling soldiers for a time to resist the ordinary causes of disease. In August, 1857, a body of soldiers was despatched from Dinapore to Arrah, partly to avenge the disaster to which allusion has already been made, and partly to relieve the small force that was besieged at the latter place. The rainy season was then at its height. The men were for upwards of twenty days employed in marching, or in fighting their Sepoy enemies. During the day and during the night they were without shelter of any kind. Fortunately, the military operations were successful. Had they been otherwise, disease to an alarming extent would doubtless have appeared among the troops, exposed as they were to drenching rain, fierce sunshine, great bodily fatigue, irregular and badly-cooked meals, want of regular sleep, and other hardships incidental to expeditions such as that in which they were engaged. But although at the time, while the excitement of military service enabled the men, as it always does, to undergo fatigues and hardships that under other circumstances would be impossible, no sooner was this moral stimulus permitted to subside, as it did on the return of the de-

* We now allude to *round s ot.*

tachment to the comparative ease and comfort of barrack life, than severe sickness attacked the majority, carrying off a very large proportion. The disease that unquestionably proved most intractable was dysentery of the hæmorrhagic type; but of this more will be said in its proper place. In circumstances such as those in which this detachment was placed, the ration of ardent spirits authorized by the regulations of the service to be issued to the soldiers is, in my opinion, to be recommended as a sanitary measure; for, however prejudicial undiluted spirits may be at other times, there is no doubt that to soldiers—wet, hungry, and exhausted—the dram of rum, by the direct stimulus it imparts, decreases their liability to diseases of a debilitating nature, to which these depressing conditions predispose them. It must be understood that it is only under particular conditions of service such as have been enumerated that the ration of spirits to soldiers is advocated; and I may here observe that the views expressed on the subject have received ample confirmation in the reports of more recent field operations. Among such I may mention the expedition to Bhootan, several medical officers connected with which were led to believe that a moderate allowance of spirits acted as a protection against malaria in that most malarious country; and during that to Magdala, the medical officers have recorded the circumstance that after the soldiers had been some days deprived of their stimulant an evident deterioration in health began, attended by diarrhœa, and inability to completely digest and assimilate their food. It is further borne out by the experience of American medical officers during the late civil war in that country, as related by Dr. Hammond in his work on military hygiene.

For several weeks the regiment to which my present remarks more immediately refer had to hold itself at all times prepared for a sudden attack to be made by the rebel Sepoys upon the station which it occupied, and for the very probable contingency of an attack on the part of the native inhabitants of a neighbouring city,* in which were situated the Government opium stores, containing a quantity of that drug valued at two millions sterling; thus its duties for that time were very severe. It moreover became necessary to locate a company of men in a close, ill-ventilated building connected with those stores, and the result was that in an incredibly short space of time a large proportion became attacked with hæmorrhagic dysentery and phagedenic ulcers, to both of which diseases they had doubtless been rendered predisposed by previous exposure and fatigue, but which were directly excited by the insanitary conditions into which they were thrown.

As the principal loss sustained by the regiment occurred during the three first months in which it was occupied in the operations against the mutineers, it may be interesting, in a medical point of view, to record the amount of that loss during July, August, and September.

From the records of the hospital, it appears that the decrease in the regiment, exclusive of the 47 killed as already mentioned, included—seven died of cholera, five of hepatitis, and 18 from various other causes of a miscellaneous nature; thus giving a total of 77 deaths in three months in an average aggregate strength for the same period of 837; or, to state the rates of mortality still more explicitly, an average rate of upwards of 36 per cent. per annum. During the same three months, no fewer than 426 cases of disease and injuries were treated in hospital, instead of 311 in the same period immediately preceding.

During the months of October, November, and December, the duties were considerably lightened by the presence of detachments of others sent for that purpose. The hot and rainy seasons had gone; the most healthy period of the year set in; and, as might be expected, the numbers treated and died in hospital materially diminished, the former being 330 and the latter 5.

* Patna.

From the latter part of December to 31st March, 1858, the entire regiment was employed on field service. During that time it marched a distance of upwards of four hundred miles, going to and returning from Lucknow, at the siege of which it took a prominent part. For some time it occupied a standing camp; several times it was engaged with the rebels; and finally made continuous forced marches to the relief of Azimghur, where they were besieging a small British force. Thus, then—in quarters, on field service, during a siege, in an unfortunate surprise, and in a rapid military advance—the 10th Regiment was employed during the first year of the Indian mutiny in nearly every variety of service that infantry can be called upon to perform.

The sanitary condition of the troops while employed on those different services was good, the severity and prevalence of disease being considerably less than in quarters. Unquestionably, the regularity of the life the soldiers were under the necessity of leading, the want of opportunity to indulge to any great extent in drunkenness—that saddest bane of the army—more than compensated for the effects of exposure and fatigue to which they were subjected. I may mention, however, that during some months embracing the hot season of 1858, when the regiment was on field service, and when the summer heat ranged to 116° F. in the shade, the men imperfectly supplied with changes of clothes and with tents, they suffered in health to a great extent. Tired and exhausted as they were on such occasions after long marches, they were unable to obtain that amount of rest and sleep that was necessary to renovate and refresh their energies. The closeness and heat of the atmosphere almost completely banished sleep from them as they lay on a pallet of straw, or had not even that substitute for a bed. The powers, thus prevented from recovering from the depression of the previous day, were still further lowered by the march and exposure, and, it might be, the attack on the morrow. Appetite next began to fail. The ordinary rations, coarsely cooked as they necessarily were, no longer were eaten with relish. There was indifference, then absolute loathing felt towards them; and thus, while duty and climate continued to exercise their depressing effects, the system obtained no support, because food was almost entirely eschewed.

Added to these, the chilopoietic functions became deranged; secretion of bile, at one time checked, at another became inordinate; irregularity of the bowels was the result—at times constipation, but more frequently diarrhœa—which reduced the remaining strength with marvellous rapidity. The ratio of attacks of diarrhœa and dysentery increased; fevers of more or less severity became more numerous; and giddiness and congestive headaches indicated, even in the absence of more severe symptoms, the effects of continued exposure to the terrific sun during May and June.

On service in India, troops are seldom deprived of their ordinary quantity of vegetables. During almost the whole of our operations potatoes were served out to the soldiers, but, as a matter of course, no variety in kind of vegetable. Fruit was not obtainable, and although no actual outbreak of scorbutus or purpura occurred, yet in not a few instances the deprivation of fruit produced a very distinct effect upon them. In some officers so distinctly was this the case, that the desire for fruit actually amounted to a perfect craving; the teeth became coated with tartar; and when at last a supply of mangoes, grapes, leechees, and peaches was brought to camp, these were devoured with an avidity and in quantities scarcely credible. Not only did no evil result follow, but in many instances the attacks of diarrhœa became less urgent, and our bodily sensations plainly told us that a want previously felt by the system had been supplied.

Although, under ordinary circumstances, the means of providing for wounded soldiers during a campaign are probably better than they are in any other country, nevertheless circumstances may in rare instances occur in which the wounded cannot be given the advantages of those arrangements. An example of this occurred in July and August, 1867, on which occasion many of the soldiers who were wounded could not receive hospital treatment till some days afterwards. The condition of some, especially those suffering from injuries of the more important bones, was deplorable. Extensive suppuration, discharges of extremely offensive matter, mortification, and the occurrence of maggots were found in all; and what rendered matters little better than they were, even with those conditions, was the fact that in the hospital at Dinapore, being filled as it was with wounded men, hospital gangrene made its appearance among them in a manner familiar only in the days of the Peninsular war. Of the hospital attendants, it too often happened that they were in no way qualified for the duties required of them. Not only were they natives of the country, with all the inherent apathy and indifference to the value of life which characterize the race to which they belonged, but they had no training whatever for their vocation; so that, except for the few soldiers who, under the exigencies of the occasion, could be spared to assist their wounded comrades, the latter were very badly off. Some attempt has, it is true, been made of late years to remedy this very sad state of affairs, but it has, I fear, not yet advanced to maturity.

The nature of the injuries usually met with in Indian warfare will best be illustrated by some examples of those that came under observation during the mutiny of the Sepoys in 1857-8. The simplicity of the treatment for the most part employed on that occasion will no doubt strike the reader; yet it is apparent that with the cleanliness and free exposure to the air that are practised, and are inseparable from active service in that country, the condition of the subjects of such injuries is in many respects far preferable while in the field to what they are after being admitted into some hospitals, as those buildings existed in connection with permanent barracks at the time to which I refer.

For the sake of convenience I would arrange wounds that came under notice on that occasion according to their nature and the tissues implicated, offering such remarks as may seem to be demanded, namely :—

A. Superficial.—The following cases will, it is believed, be sufficient to illustrate the character, progress, and treatment of the slightest description of gunshot wounds met with in field service, that is, those that only implicate the cuticle.

King, 37th Foot, was, on 29th of July, 1857, wounded by a bullet, which having passed through the left arm superficially, left as it were a bridge of skin over the channel formed by its progress. The vitality of the portion of skin that had been left seems to have been destroyed, as it speedily sloughed, the sphacelated portion separating on 9th of August, after which granulation progressed favourably, and the wound healed in fifty-three days. The applications varied. Cold water dressing was in the first instance applied ; afterwards poultices, solution of acetate of lead and opium, simple dressing, with for a time adhesive plaster to stimulate the surface, and again cold water.

Bosworth, 37th Foot, was on the same occasion wounded in the left thigh. A bullet entered its outer aspect below the hip-joint, and running superficially downwards and outwards, a distance of four inches and a half, escaped. Very profuse discharge took place from the track thus made ; but under the application of poultices in the first instance, and then of cold water, the wound completely healed in thirty-one days from the date of its receipt.

Murray, 10th Foot, while advancing on the fort of Dowrarah, was struck by a bullet which ran along the top of the left shoulder, tearing a channel through the cuticle posterior to the acromion process. There was no *shock*. Cold water dressing was applied, and on the fourth day afterwards a line of demarcation had begun to form between the thin layer of sloughed tissues below the track of the missile and the healthy parts. Six days afterwards it had completely separated, leaving a somewhat extensive but clean granulating surface. The edges were then as much as possible drawn together by adhesive straps; simple dressing was applied, and under these measures healing steadily proceeded.

Remarks.—With reference to these cases I would observe that the two men first named were not admitted until the second day afterwards; that they were treated in hospital at Dinapore, the building being not only extremely ill-adapted for its purpose, but at the time crowded with wounded, the remnant of the unfortunate force that was surprised at Arrah. Added to these circumstances was that of the rainy season being at its height, and the atmosphere damp, hot, and consequently depressing. The building was, moreover, from its construction, unsuited for thorough ventilation, and cleanliness was extremely difficult to maintain with only a native establishment. It is therefore evident that their subjects were placed in the most unfavourable circumstances that they could be.

B. Muscular.—Curry, 37th Foot, was at Arrah wounded by a bullet, which having entered below the middle of the left clavicle and passed outwards and downwards, escaped through the deltoid muscle. The bone was uninjured; there occurred no hæmorrhage, and the wound appeared to implicate no tissue of importance. Under the application of cold water dressing, it completely healed in thirty-one days, and at the end of that time the power of the arm remained unimpaired.

Tawney, 37th Foot, at the same time received a bullet in the right leg, through which it passed from behind, forward between the tibia and fibula, but without injuring either of these bones, or destroying a vessel. A tubular slough in due time formed and separated. Cold water dressing was alone applied, and in thirty-five days after the injury he returned to his duty, the opening of exit having been the first to close.

C. Encysted Bullets.—Sherlock, 10th Foot, was wounded by the mutineers at Benares. The bullet entered about he centre of the left hip, about two inches below the crest of the ilium, and was believed to have become firmly impacted in the bone. For some time he was treated in the detachment hospital by Assistant-surgeon Tulloch,* and only reached head-quarters upwards of four months after having received the injury. At a consultation which was then held it was considered advisable to make no attempt at recovering the missile. A sinus then existed, but it gradually healed up, and in six weeks more the external opening had entirely closed. He was sent to England as an invalid.

D. Bones of Lower Extremity—Patella.—McCormick, 37th Foot, sustained a gunshot wound across the left patella. On admission it did not appear that that bone was anything more than grazed by the bullet; the wound, however, became rapidly painful, its edges swollen, and much constitutional disturbance set in. A week afterwards it became evident that the patella had been comminuted. A large portion of it was found to be loose and was accordingly removed. The limb had at first been left loose, water dressing being applied to the wound; subsequently it was secured by a splint, leeches were applied to the knee, ipecacuan and James's powder given internally, with cream of tartar drinks. The pain and constitutional disturbance continued, and when seen by me nineteen days after the receipt of the injury he was suffering severely. I resolved to amputate the limb, but a severe accession of pyrexia occurring, the operation had to be postponed till the following day; meantime the patient had an apoplectic seizure and died. Examination of the limb discovered a large quantity of offensive pus and gas welling from the knee-joint, which was then seen to have been extensively injured.

The remarks appended to this case state that death probably arose from pyæmia, and that had primary amputation been performed, the man's life would in all proba-

---

* Now Surgeon, 1st Battalion 11th Foot.

bility have been saved. It may be illustrative in these respects.

Of Femur.—Carey, 10th Foot, nine days before admission, had been shot by a musket bullet through the left femur. The bone was extensively shattered ; the parts in and around the wound suppurating, disorganized, and offensive. Amputation was as a last resort performed, but too late. The operation took place on the tenth day after the receipt of the injury, but on the succeeding, the patient sank and died exhausted. This man had been carried from place to place after the receipt of his wound, the want of appliances putting it out of the power of the medical officer to do almost anything to relieve him. It is not often that such circumstances occur in India, but sometimes unfortunately they do.

Remarks.—Had primary amputation been performed in this case according to the principle laid down by Guthrie, it is more than probable that the life of this soldier might have been saved.

E. Bones of Upper Extremity—Forearm.—Bolan, 5th Foot, was wounded by a bullet which entered the forearm a little above the wrist, fracturing the radius. He received no hospital treatment for seven days afterwards, and when admitted had considerable swelling of the hand and inflammation around the seat of injury. Leeches, followed by fomentations, were applied ; the untoward symptoms were at once subdued. The limb was then placed in a splint, cold water dressing applied, nourishing diet allowed, and at the expiration of twelve days from his admission he was able to proceed to join his own regiment.

Knott, 37th Foot, admitted with a gunshot wound, destroying the left radius and ulna, rendering amputation necessary. Maggots appeared in the stump, but were destroyed by turpentine, after which, under the use of cold water, and latterly of simple cerate, granulation and cicatrization took place favourably.

Walsh, 10th Foot, had on the same occasion received a gunshot wound in the forearm. The bullet had entered from behind, four inches below the elbow-joint, fractured the radius, and escaped by a large opening in front. No fragment of bone had come away; the wound looked clean, having from the date of its receipt been treated by cold water. The hospital into which he was brought had at the time been crowded with wounded men, and the building itself ill ventilated. A tendency to hospital gangrene made its appearance in both wounds about three weeks afterwards, and when to all appearance they were progressing favourably. His conditions were improved as far as was practicable; opium applied locally, calomel and opium given internally. The threatened disease was averted, and he recovered with but loss of power in the hand and wrist.

Humerus.—Lieut. St. John, 10th Foot, during a night attack between the 11th and 12th of May, 1858, was wounded by a musket bullet, which entered at the front of the left arm about its middle, passed directly through the humerus, fracturing and splintering it severely. The posterior opening was very large and torn; there was a second aperture, as if it had been produced by a spicula of fractured bone; and as the missile escaped, it struck the side, abrading the skin. The power and sensation of ring and little finger were gone; the others retained a little of both. The pulse beat naturally at the wrist. The arm was put up in splints; cold water applied. Suppuration attended by some fever followed. On the 19th, the discharge was very copious; there was a good deal of œdema of the forearm, but the wound looked healthy.

The progress of this case was satisfactory; both the wounds healed, cold water having been the only application used, with the exception of poultices during a few days to encourage the commencement of suppuration. Union took place, but the hand remained powerless; the general health was good; he was sent on sick leave to England in July, and a year afterwards, on the return of the regiment, joined it at Plymouth, but with the hand permanently disabled.

Captain Cator, 10th Foot, was, on 14th March, 1858, during the operations connected with the capture of Lucknow, wounded in the left arm by a musket bullet, which entered about the middle of the limb, between the biceps and the humerus, passed backwards, and making its escape posteriorly by a very large and ragged opening, the humerus being fractured in its progress. When seen, immediately on the receipt of the wound, the front opening was wide; the hæmorrhage from the posterior was considerable; sensation and motion were destroyed in the ring and little finger, and partially so in the middle one.

This officer having been so unfortunate as to have had the power of flexing the right elbow destroyed by a wound received in the Crimea, it was deemed advisable to hold a consultation on his case, the result of which was that, in accordance with the principles laid down by Guthrie, an attempt should be made to save the limb. On the 16th, irritative fever set in, and was treated by diaphoretics; cold water dressing was applied to the wound, and he was transferred to the field hospital, where the wound ultimately healed; the fracture in the humerus reunited, but the loss of power and sensation in the fingers remained permanently destroyed.

Shoulder.—Taylor, 37th Foot, received a bullet which entered near the acromial end of the right scapula, and was cut out posteriorly opposite the head of the humerus. The part of the scapula through which the missile passed was comminuted; but no spicula came away at the time. The discharge became very fetid, and partial sloughing occurred of the parts around the posterior opening. Much pain was complained of along the whole arm, and considerable swelling of the hand supervened. Slight irritative fever made its appearance, but was soon checked by febrifuges. The local applications consisted only of poultices and cold water dressing, used alternatively as each seemed to be indicated; afterwards solution of lead and opium during the day; ointment of the same at night. Thirty days after admission, and thirty-one after the receipt of the wound, two small spiculæ came away from the posterior wound, after a night of unusual suffering along the median nerve by the patient. Other small pieces, evidently of the scapula, subsequently came away, and the opening of exit was then the first to heal. The history of the case contains a remark to the effect that the attack of pyrexia, under which the patient laboured, seems to have been induced by the tainted atmosphere of the hospital. It would seem, however, that on its being subdued recovery progressed favourably; the man, although deprived of the use of the arm, retained good health, and at the expiration of eighty-two days from the injury was invalided.

F.—Of the Neck.—Swift, 10th Foot, was wounded by a bullet which entered at the root of the neck on the left side, passed backwards and downwards, and escaped at the left side of the spinal column, having traversed close to the outside of the sterno-mastoid muscle, through the trapezius, and escaping just above the superior angle of the scapula. He was reported to have expectorated or vomited about a pint of blood, and for some days afterwards to have spat up small quantities. Extensive ecchymosis occurred around the wound, but there was no constitutional disturbance. The progress of the case under cold water dressing was satisfactory; both wounds healed favourably, that of ingress first. Some stiffness of the neck remained; but as hospital gangrene had appeared in hospital, he was sent to barracks, and made a complete recovery.

G.—Of the Face.—Nolan, 10th Foot, was wounded by a bullet in the left cheek. It entered directly over the left sterno-mastoid, injured slightly the lower jaw, and destroyed several of the posterior teeth; then lodged and was cut out behind the parotid duct. Extensive inflammation and suppuration followed; the matter burrowed down the neck, but was given egress by a counter opening. Seventeen days after the wound small spiculæ of bone from the injured jaw came away; others continued to do so for some time afterwards. Under cold water applications, and then simple dressing, the case progressed favourably.

The wound of entrance was the first to heal; the others granulated favourably, and on the sixty-fifth day of the injury he returned to barracks.

O'Neal, 37th Foot, was wounded by a bullet which entered at the lower part of the back of the head, below and close to the right mastoid process, passed directly forwards, knocking out the two posterior molar teeth of the upper jaw, and lodged in the mouth, from which, together with the teeth, it was spat out. The man was stunned by the shot. He fell, and on attempting to rise, fell again several times before assistance reached him. On being brought to hospital, cold water dressing was applied, and from that time forward not a bad symptom appeared. In twenty-two days after the receipt of the wound that in the mouth had healed; on the 27th of the same month that of entrance had closed, and on the thirty-first day of the injury he returned to duty. No other application than cold water, and then simple dressing, is noted as having been used; and no medicine was given internally.

H.—Of the Skull.—Giffard, 37th Foot, was, on 29th July, 1857, shot in the head. The bullet struck over the apex of the lambdoid suture, made in the scalp a ragged irregular opening of two inches and a-half in length, laying bare and denuding the outer table of periosteum, but apparently causing no fracture. From that date to 7th August the man complained of inability to sleep, but had no constitutional disturbance. A profuse discharge occurred, and severe pain in the wound was from time to time complained of. Up to the 11th cold water dressing was alone applied. On that day leeches were applied around the seat of injury, inflammation having run somewhat high, and being only for the time relieved by them. During the few ensuing days he was drowsy; the pulse laborious; the pupils dilated. On the 16th maggots appeared in the wound, but were destroyed by the application of turpentine. Calomel, in combination with James's powder or Dover's powder, was given at short intervals, and in small doses; poultices, cold water, and simple dressing being applied as indicated. On the 20th, the first decided improvement was apparent, the inflammation around the wound having moderated. On the 27th, his expression was much improved ; he was cool ; wound discharging freely ; the pus healthy ; a piece of dead bone was perceptible at the bottom of the wound ; and for the first time a desire for food was expressed.

The notes of the case record that from this date a steady improvement took place, it being remarkable, considering the extensive nature of the injury. The greater part of the wound granulated steadily, although at one point the dead bone could still be seen. By the 16th of September he had taken on flesh, and was walking about the ward. It was then found that suppuration had taken place under the scalp, in a direction towards the occiput. The pus was then regularly pressed up towards the wound, where it escaped, and poultices applied. On the 11th October, a counter opening had, however, to be made. The dead portion of bone gradually became loosened ; and on 6th December, a ragged piece, consisting of both tables, two inches and a-half long and one inch broad, was extracted, the long axis being across the occiput in the track of the wound.

The patient did well, and was sent to England with the invalids of the season.

Allen, 10th Foot, was, at Sooltanpore, struck by a grape-shot at the junction of the occipital with the two parietal bones, the injury chiefly affecting the left side of the head. A portion of bone nearly two inches square was depressed by the missile as it glanced off, and the man when picked up laboured under all the ordinary symptoms of compressed brain. No trephine was at the time available, but by means of a free incision through the scalp, and a small saw, a triangular piece of skull was removed, so as to admit an elevator ; and thus, within half an hour of the wound being inflicted, the depressed and comminuted portions were removed. The scalp was drawn together, and cold water dressing applied. On the succeeding day he spoke, and manifested other signs of returning sensibility. The pupils were natural as to size, but contracted sluggishly, and there was ptosis of the right eyelid. On the 25th, after an unusually long march, he was found evidently worse. He had during the night and earlier part of the day been picking the bedclothes in his dooly, but when seen towards afternoon lay supine. There was no stertor; pulse was small and rapid; skin moist, and of natural temperature; the features contracted. On the following day he died, and then examination revealed the fact that the fracture had extended through the parietal bone down towards the base of the skull. The exterior of the dura mater was covered with clotted matter, and softened. The surface of the brain within the arachnoid, over the occipital region, was covered with effused blood, and in some parts the cortical part had already become softened.

I. Of the Chest.—Superficial.—Andrews, 37th Foot, was struck by a bullet immediately below the right nipple. The missile passed backwards, and escaped at the angle of the fifth rib without inflicting a fracture. The "shock" of the injury was severe. The seat of the wound became very irritable, and considerable constitutional irritation supervened. Poultices to the wound, with Dover's powder, quinine, and cinchona bark internally, subdued those symptoms; simple dressing and lead lotion were alternately applied to the wounds, and recovery was completed in fifty-one days.

Complicated.—Cleary, 10th Foot, was, during the action at Sooltanpore, struck by a grape-shot over the region of the breast. The missile, having penetrated the skin, slipped down to near the ensiform cartilage of the sternum, from which point it was extracted by incision. Immediately on receiving the wound, the man expectorated blood to a considerable extent; but it did not appear that any rib was fractured. At the time he was treated by tartrate of antimony internally, and by application of cold water to the wound. On the following day, his symptoms were favourable; expectoration had decreased; he was therefore ordered calomel and opium to guard against probable inflammation, and the treatment was continued for some days. On the tenth after receiving the injury, he suffered severely from pain at a point a little lower than that where the bullet had been extracted. There was much oppression of breathing; pulse was small and quick; expectoration not copious, clear and frothy. He was at this time distinctly under the influence of the calomel that had been administered. On the thirteenth day, while the regiment was on the march, profuse bleeding suddenly took place from the wound, which was accordingly enlarged with a view to secure any arterial opening that might be found; none was discovered, but it was then found that the sternal portion of the seventh rib had been fractured. Pressure and styptic applications were employed, but for some days the hæmorrhage continued to recur. A consultation was held, but the point could not be determined whether the bleeding proceeded from the internal mammary or from the intercostal artery. The alternative of passing a ligature round the portion of the rib, in the hope of thus securing the latter, was had recourse to; but as our after movements necessitated his transfer to a field hospital, the subsequent history of the case is not forthcoming. Notwithstanding that it is incomplete, however, it is deemed interesting in its way, as illustrating a particular kind of injury met with on service; and it may be observed that somewhat similar ones are related in Ranking's Half-Yearly Abstract to December, 1856, and in the *Edinburgh Medical Journal* for May, 1856. Guthrie, in his Commentaries, page 519, edition of 1855, acknowledges the great difficulty there is in treating wounds of this nature.

K.—Through the Sacrum.—Walker, 10th Foot, while swimming a nullah at Arrah, received a gunshot wound. The bullet entered the centre of the sacrum; and on his being brought to hospital two days afterwards, the left lower extremity was found to be paralysed, and he unable to void urine. A large opening indicated the entrance of the bullet; the finger discovered the sacrum bare and rough, but the further progress of the missile could not be traced. There seemed at first to be very little constitutional disturbance, but during the night after his admission he sank into a low state, requiring the very free administration of stimulants. This condition was but temporary, however; he rallied, and up to the thirteenth day after the injury he seemed remarkably well. From that time, however, the powers gradually succumbed; a profuse fetid discharge took place from the wound; he became emaciated; bed-sores appeared on the prominent parts; the penis, from having been so long a time resting in the urinal, became excoriated, and existence became a burthen. Yet it was not until the thirty-third day after the injury that he died. Post-mortem examination revealed the fact that the anterior part of the sacrum was shattered and comminuted in a frightful manner. The bullet had formed a canal for itself, and rested on the body of the fourth lumbar vertebra in front. The lumbar muscles were separated from their attachments by quantities of suppuration; and the origin of the vesical twigs of the lumbar plexus being destroyed accounted for the paralysis of the viscus.

L.—Penetrating the Intestine.—Macartney, 10th Foot, was, on 12th May, 1858, wounded in action at Chitowrah. The bullet made its entrance between the 10th and 11th ribs, in a line above the anterior spine of the ilium, and seems to have passed downwards and backwards, escaping an inch and a-half to the left of the spinous processes of the first and second lumbar vertebræ, close to the crest of the ilium. At the same time he received a wound from a second bullet, which, entering on the outer aspect of the left arm about its middle, passed inwards completely through it. He was struck down insensible by these injuries, remained in that state some time, and when brought to hospital was suffering from a considerable degree of "shock." On the following day, symptoms of peritonitis set in, attended by severe vomiting of bilious matter, and the contents of the large intestine were discovered to be escaping from the wound posteriorly. On the 14th, these symptoms had already begun to moderate, and some fæces were voided per anum. On the morning of the 15th, there was a very free fæcal discharge from the posterior wound; considerable tympanitis; skin moist, and of natural temperature; face free from anxiety; pulse soft, small, and slow. He complained much of thirst, vomited much bile, but was not restless. Tongue coated with bilious coloured fur; bowels not moved naturally since the previous day, but very profuse fæcal discharge from the wound, it being livid, dark, and offensive. He had from the first occurrence of peritonitis been treated with mercurials. The gums were now tender; he had, however, calomel in quarter-grain doses every three hours, the diet being restricted to tea and bread. The notes of the case, taken at the time, state that it was remarkable how little he suffered. All the symptoms of peritonitis had disappeared by the 19th, but he still continued to vomit bilious matter. The greater part of the fæces were voided by the wound, but some also by the natural passage. The skin and pulse were natural. On the 21st he was moved from the field to Arrah, where a temporary hospital had been established; and when again seen, eight days afterwards, the fæces had ceased to flow from the posterior opening, and the anterior was healing favourably. From this time till the 19th of June the progress of the case was in all respects favourable. By that time the anterior opening had completely healed; the posterior remained a granulating surface. He was then carried with the regiment towards Dinapore, a distance of about twenty-five miles, and which he reached on the 20th. Soon afterwards he was attacked with slight pyrexia, which however was speedily subdued under treatment; the state of the bowels continued variable, but they were generally relaxed. On the 21st July, the posterior opening, which had for some days been healed, presented an ulcerated spot, and on the same afternoon some fæces came away; there was no pyrexia; no pain was complained of, and the state of the bowels was natural. He seems to have remained in much the same state till towards the end of September, when the mornings and evenings having begun to become slightly cool, his health began to improve. The posterior wound at times gave exit to the contents of the bowel, and he was at times troubled with pain in the abdomen. On the 11th October, he proceeded as an invalid *en route* to England.

Gunshot Wound of Uncertain Nature.—It is scarcely to be anticipated that a wound inflicted by a bullet should in any case be so dubious in its nature as to set diagnosis at defiance. All writers on injuries of this nature relate instances in which the course of bullets has been extremely eccentric ; but in that about to be related, although the course of the missile was to a certain extent sufficiently apparent, the actual degree of injury, and all the tissues affected by it, remained undiscovered.

Teehan, 10th Foot, was, at Lucknow, wounded by a bullet in the loins. The missile entered a little to the right of the first lumbar vertebra, but its course could not be traced, although a free opening was made with that view; the right lower extremity was powerless as regards motion, but sensation was unaffected. After a few days the slough which formed in the wound separated, leaving a clean opening, and then there seemed reason to believe that the bullet had not lodged, as was at first suspected. He had to be sent to a field hospital afterwards, owing to the regiment having to pursue the rebels, and when, five months afterwards he rejoined, it was found that although the power over the limb was considerably restored, and the wound had completely healed, he was totally unfit for the duties of a soldier, and was accordingly invalided.

Burns.—Some general remarks having already been made on this class of injuries as met with on service in India, I submit an illustrative case.

Akers, whose name has been already mentioned, was, at Lucknow, blown up by the explosion of gunpowder. When brought to the hospital tents shortly after the accident, the cuticle was found destroyed over the whole face and front of the neck, the eyes being uninjured save that they were considerably suffused with blood. The cuticle of the hands and wrists hung in shreds, curled up and shrivelled; that of the feet, entire lower extremities, nates, genitals, and pubis was in a similar state—thus much more than one-third of his entire surface was implicated. When first seen in hospital he was shivering, and complained of feeling cold; the pulse was small, and he was suffering from intense pain. The injured parts were dressed with Carron oil, and a large dose of brandy with opium was administered. It was soon afterwards discovered that the parts where the injuries were most extensive were completely destitute of sensation; those less so being still intensely painful. Great irritability of the stomach and continual vomiting speedily set in, and continued till he died, exhausted, on the fourth day after receiving his injuries.

This is a type of other cases of severe burn that came under observation, in all of which the persons injured suffered from sensation of great cold; some had intense thirst, others expressed a desire to sleep; but all were speedily seized with frequent vomiting and great irritability of the stomach.

Hospital Gangrene.—The following cases rather illustrate the measures by which this terrible malady may be checked at its onset than its own destructive progress; they are, however, it is hoped, not the less interesting on this account.

Akers, 10th Foot, was wounded by a bullet which passed through the right thigh, from without inwards, entering about the middle and escaping near Hunter's canal, but apparently not penetrating the limb below the fascia. Little constitutional disturbance occurred, and for fifteen days after the receipt of the wound it progressed favourably under the application of cold water and poultices alternately. From that time his state was reported as not having been so satisfactory, and the wound not to have continued to progress. On the twenty-third day after the injury he was found restless, feverish, and irritable. The openings of entrance and exit had become deep, cupped, and painful; the neighbouring parts were red, swollen, and very irritable; a clear serous liquid oozed from both wounds. Opium was now applied to the wounds, calomel in two-grain doses combined with one grain of opium was administered every three hours; the bedding was changed; the vicinity of the bed in which he lay thoroughly cleaned and whitewashed. In two days the characters of the sores had undergone a favourable change; the local and constitutional symptoms had given way; the phagedenic action was checked at its commencement. On the twenty-ninth day the administration of calomel and opium was omitted; an ointment of acetate of lead and opium was applied to the sores, the appearance of which was that of tardy ulcers. Under great attention to diet, cleanliness, nourishing food, and stimulating applications, he gradually recovered, to be subsequently killed by a burn at Lucknow.

Kenny, 10th Foot, was shot by a bullet, which passed through and through the muscular tissues of the middle of the thigh without inflicting any other injury. He had to walk eight miles after receiving the wound, and when admitted into hospital manifested little or no disturbance of the system. Under cold-water dressing the wound did well, and continued so till the twenty-fifth day after the injury, when the wound of entrance suddenly assumed a cup-shaped form, became excessively irritable, the surrounding parts swollen and painful, and the patient himself attacked by pyrexia. The surface of both wounds was at once covered with opium; calomel and opium were given in small doses every three hours; great attention was paid to cleanliness. The phagedenic action did not from that time advance; the sores at once began to improve in appearance, and under the application of lead and opium lotion they healed; the man being sent to duty sixty-one days after receiving his wound.

Mortification.—The case about to be related under this head is one of extremely rare occurrence. Sloughing of the parts directly injured by bullets is common enough, and in fact forms an ordinary stage in the progress of such cases; so also is gangrene of the distal portion of a limb in cases of destruction of the principal vessels, but the following is in its nature very different from either of these.

Mr. Venables, a civilian, forty-five years of age, and twenty-seven years in India, was, on the 15th April, 1858, wounded during an attack on the Sepoys, near Azimghur. A bullet struck the outer aspect of the lower extremity of the left ulna, fractured the bone without entering the joint, ran up the side of the forearm, and was cut out near the elbow. There was at the time nothing in the injury to occasion anxiety, and the medical officer by whom he was attended therefore merely put the arm in a splint, and loosely bandaged it. On the morning of the 17th Mr. Venables had a shivering fit, succeeded by the different stages of what seemed an ordinary attack of intermittent fever, to which for years he had at intervals been subject. While the pyrexia lasted he was therefore treated by diaphoretics and effervescents. On the evening of that day he complained of feeling that the rings which he wore on the fingers of the injured hand were tight; they were accordingly taken off. He also complained of diffused pain in the left shoulder, but somehow or other no further notice seems to have been taken of the state of the arm till the morning of the 18th, when it was discovered to be cold, black, and covered with phlyctenæ; the arm, from the elbow-joint to the shoulder, was swollen, and presenting all the modifications of green, yellow, and blue; under the clavicle distinct emphysema was detected; the pulse was rapid and hard; face flushed, general manner excited, and he was generally delirious, although still capable at times of collecting his ideas. It was obviously too late to do anything effective in this case. Brandy and opium were given, and at three a.m. of 19th he died. The heat of the weather was at the time very great, and although his body was interred the same afternoon, the state to which decomposition had advanced was horrible to look at. His habits had been free, but his general health was what in India is considered good, intermittent fever being held as of no account. With reference to this case, my object is not to remark upon the treatment pursued, but to bring it forward as illustrating a complication which, although by no means common, at times accompanies gunshot wounds in India.

Traumatic Tetanus.—This terrible complication is fortunately of comparatively rare occurrence after wounds on service in India. The following is, however, a very illustrative case of its progress and termination :—

Byrnes, 10th Foot, on 28th July, 1857, received a gunshot wound which passed through the upper part of the left thigh, without injuring the femur. He arrived at the regimental hospital the following day, and by that time considerable inflammation had set in. Leeches were applied around the wound; their bites bled very freely, and for some days thereafter he seemed free from constitutional disturbance. On the 4th August the pain and sense of tension at the wound were described as very great. On the following day these symptoms were increased, a thin bloody discharge oozed from the wound, restlessness was great, skin was hot, pulse rapid and tongue white; at four p.m. of that date he suffered from pain and stiffness in the jaws, which were nearly closed; he could with an effort swallow; pain was complained of in the back of the neck; the head was bent backwards, and the features were distorted. Towards evening accessions of spasms occurred in distinct paroxysms, at intervals of ten to twenty minutes; the body on each occasiou was drawn violently backwards, the sufferer uttering loud screams from agony. Deglutition soon became almost impossible; the abdomen felt distended, hard, and painful; pulse 100, full; surface warm and dry; urine was voided naturally. On the 6th, the conditions continued with little alteration; surface had become cool, and pulse sank to 90. In the afternoon of that day an aggravation of the symptoms took place, and injury of the sciatic nerve was suspected. The tetanic spasms increased in severity and frequency. Chloroform was liberally administered, in addition to the other remedies usual in such cases; no benefit was obtained, however. He gradually became unable to expectorate the phlegm that rapidly accumulated in his bronchii, and during the evening he died in great agony. No post-mortem examination seems to have been performed.

Dysentery.

It may safely be asserted that in no disease so much as dysentery has the introduction of sanitary improvement exerted so marked an influence; the characters of that affection as it is now met with but faintly approaching those by which it was distinguished when it was the custom to crowd our soldiers together in imperfectly ventilated Indian barracks. In former days, this disease as it prevailed at some of our stations along the banks of the Ganges in Lower Bengal, was more fatal in its individual attacks than cholera, and numerically more prevalent than the latter; thus, while statistics show that during the thirteen years subsequent to 1842, the rate of occurrence of dysentery among our soldiery to have been 10·57 per cent. of strength, and that of mortality by it 11·47 per cent. of those treated, we learn by the Army Blue Book for 1866, that during that year the admissions by this affection in both its acute and chronic form were only at the rate of 3·80 per 100 strength, and of deaths 4·52 of those treated. I shall have occasion in the course of these notes to give some *cases* illustrative of the disease as it formerly prevailed among our troops in that country, and I venture to believe that whatever credit may now be justly assumed as belonging to the method of treating it, as compared with that formerly followed, yet the characters of the disease are now very different from what they previously were; improved sanitation having changed if not the type, at least the alarming severity with which in former days the malady made its attacks. When, for example, the 10th Regiment occupied the citadel of Lahore, soon after the subjugation of the Punjab, the men having been crowded together in rooms imperfectly ventilated and lighted, this disease prevailed so severely and extensively among them as to appear almost as an epidemic, at the same time that the officers, who were better accommodated, were almost exempt from it.

Number Died.	Hair.	Eyes.	Complexion.
2	Fair	Blue	Fresh
1	—	—	Fair
1	—	Grey	Fresh
1	Light	Blue	Fair
1	—	Grey	Fresh
2	Red	Blue	Fresh
1	—	Grey	Fresh
1	—	—	Fair
2	Sandy	Blue	Fresh
3	—	Grey	Fresh
2	—	—	Fair
1	—	Hazel	Fresh
11	Light Brown	Blue	Fresh
4	—	—	Fair
15	—	Grey	Fresh
1	—	Grey	Fair
1	—	Hazel	Sallow
2	—	Light Brown	Fresh
2	—	Brown	—
1	—	Dark	Fair
11	Brown	Blue	Fresh
1	—	—	Fair
1	—	—	Pale
27	—	Grey	Fresh
5	—	—	Fair
3	—	—	Sallow
4	—	Hazel	Fresh
3	—	Brown	—
1	—	—	Fair
1	—	—	Sallow
3	Dark Brown	Blue	Fresh
2	—	—	Fair
2	—	—	Dark
1	—	—	Sallow

Number Died.	Hair.	Eyes.	Complexion.
11	Dark Brown	Grey	Fresh
1	—	—	Fair
2	—	—	Sallow
1	—	—	Pale
8	—	Hazel	Fresh
2	—	—	Sallow
1	—	—	Dark
1	—	Dark Hazel	Dark
6	—	Brown	Fresh
1	Dark	Blue	Fair
2	—	Grey	Fresh
1	—	—	Pale
1	—	—	Dark
1	—	Hazel	Fair
1	—	Brown	Fresh
1	Black	Blue	—
2	—	Grey	—
1	—	—	Sallow
1	—	Hazel	Fresh
2	—	—	Dark
1	—	Brown	Fresh
1	—	—	Dark

Much has been said in regard to the coincidence of hepatitis and dysentery in the same individual. I believe such connection to be neither invariable or necessary, although in persons saturated with malaria, as many become after long residence in Lower Bengal, and in whom the dysentery assumes the hæmorrhagic type, the coincidence is very frequent. In what is called inflammatory dysentery, occurring for the most part in the upper stations of the country, the two affections may occur perfectly independent of each other, and perhaps my own experience on these points may be taken as confirming the views expressed by Sir Rainald Martin. Not only do different types of the disease prevail at stations in different parts of India, but in different years at the same station; it may be assumed, however, as a rule, that in the north-west provinces the form most frequently met with is the inflammatory, and in the Gangetic stations the hæmorrhagic. In the former, active treatment, including depletion, calomel, opium, ipecacuanha, &c., has always been found most effective, the adjuncts being fomentations, hot water enemata, &c., and restriction of diet; while in the latter the indications all point to a different *régime*, and it is to be feared are not always met by young practitioners, who do not stop to consider the cases most suited for large doses of the last-named remedy, the re-introduction of which into practice has lately attracted much attention.

Were it practicable to institute statistics on a large scale regarding the prevalence in India and other hot countries of endemic diseases according to temperament, very valuable results would be obtained; thus in the selection of young soldiers to be sent abroad, army medical officers would have it in their power, in some measure at least, to select those who were thus shown to be the least susceptible to those diseases, and to reject those who are most liable to suffer from them. With this view I prepared the preceding abstract of deaths by dysentery among soldiers of the 10th Foot in India, according to temperament, as indicated by the colour of hair, eyes, and complexion.

I regret that I was not able to collect similar information in regard to the subjects of other *zymotic* diseases; and although the above numbers are too few in themselves to justify us in drawing any conclusions from them, yet I consider that the field of inquiry which they indicate is both an important and extensive one, and one which I trust will soon be investigated.

I would select the following cases as illustrative of the two forms of the disease as met with in India, premising that in the first class only does medical treatment appear to have much power. In the latter I have employed various methods, but regret to say with poor success; nor do I think that the disease, as observed at some stations, Dinapore for example, some twelve years ago, was amenable to treatment after its characteristic symptoms had fairly set in.

a. Inflammatory Dysentery.—Joseph McDonell, 10th Foot, thirty-six years of age, fifteen in India, had for many years been a hard drinker, although for some time previous to his present admission he had become more temperate in his habits. During his Indian service he had on two occasions suffered from dysentery, and for three months prior to his admission on 31st of October, 1858, the state of his bowels had been irregular, he having been treated on two occasions on account of diarrhœa. About ten days before he applied for admission, he began to suffer from pain in the abdomen, occasional calls to stool, especially for some time after going to bed. He complained of a constant sensation of coldness in the abdomen, and of borborygmi, and these symptoms increasing in severity, he began to strain when at stool. On admission there was tenderness along the course of the colon, and in the left iliac region; the stools were scanty, consisted of slime and blood like jelly, and were attended by much straining. A dose of castor oil and tincture of opium was administered, then three grains of calomel and one of opium, to be repeated every three hours, fomentations being constantly applied to the abdomen. After he had taken eight of these pills his sensations were reported as having improved, pain had diminished, and the evacuations contained liquid fæces. The pills were omitted, but the succeeding day the symptoms became aggravated, those from which he had at first suffered returning in an increased degree. On 3rd Nov the pulse was 124, hard and wiry, calls to stool frequent, evacuations consisting almost entirely of liquid blood; there was much tenderness over the abdomen, great straining, but no heat of skin. He was now bled from the arm to sixteen ouuces, which at once reduced the pulse to 100; leeches were applied to the anus, emollient enemata administered, and poultices applied to the abdomen. On the 4th the pain was less, pulsc 84, soft; straining less urgent, but he felt very weak, and still the sensation of coldness in the abdomen continued; surface natural, tongue covered with yellow fur. Was now directed to have opium, 1 gr. m., pil., hyd. gr. ij., ipecac. gr. ij. every fourth hour, poultices and emollient enemata being repeated from time to time. On the 5th the mouth was tender, but an evident improvement was observable in all the symptoms; the evacuations were voided with less straining; consisted chiefly of mucus, only coloured with blood, but both in diminished quantity; there was less pain along the course of the colon, and it was specifically noted that no hepatic complication could be detected. At this stage the blue pill was omitted, but the ipecacuanha and opium continued as before. According to the report of the 7th, he had not been moved the previous night; the tongue had begun to clean at the tip; the mouth was better; pulse 80; all sensations improved. On the 8th he was stated to have been only once moved since the previous day, and in all other respects to have still further improved. He had now a dose consisting of ext. sennæ, ℈i.; pulv. rhœi, grs. x.; carb. magnes., grs., x.; aquæ, ℥i. His diet had been "spoon," with sago as an extra. From this date his improvement was progressive, and on 24th he was discharged to duty perfectly well.

I consider the above to be a typical case, both as to its symptoms and progress, and in regard to the treatment pursued; and although I do not purpose entering upon the consideration of the latter at length, I nevertheless, on looking back to the notes of this case, think the symptoms, as they successively arose, were directly checked by the remedies employed.

b. Hæmorrhagic.—It will be sufficient to describe the symptoms as they occurred, and briefly refer to the *post-mortem* appearances. John Brown, 10th Regiment, was admitted into the hospital at Dinapore, on 26th August, 1858. He had for years been a hard drinker, was a man of plethoric habit of body, and had only a few days before returned from pursuing the rebel Sepoys in the Jugdespore jungles, where he had been exposed to much fatigue, and almost constant wet. When admitted he was suffering from frequent purging of liquid matter containing a large proportion of bile ; there was much abdominal pain and straining, and he stated that he had become attacked with these symptoms three days previously. The remedies employed failed to check them. On the 28th he was stated to have had much straining during the preceding night, with almost constant desire to evacuate the bowels. On that day, he having had a dose of laxative medicine (rhubarb and carbonate of magnesia), a free evacuation was obtained without pain, but the matter voided had the appearance of liquid blood, without shreds. There was no abdominal pain, skin was warm, pulse soft. On the 29th he continued to void similar matters, with some streaks of feculent matter. Between that morning and the 30th, he had been moved thirteen times ; the nature of the matters voided continued as before ; there was much thirst ; tongue clean and moist ; surface natural in temperature, but red and congested, as it had been from the time of his admission. Notwithstanding the various remedies that were administered, his condition went on from bad to worse. On 31st, the report of his case stated that he had been frequently purged ; the stools like solution of blood, now containing some clots ; the state of the tongue, pulse, and skin unaltered. The frequency with which he was moved increased, and the report of 2nd Sept. states that the evacuations had a distinctly cadaverous odour ; the precise sensations complained of in the abdomen were a combination of those of emptiness and coldness, and of weight in the hypogastric region. He, moreover, complained of experiencing a peculiar feeling of sinking. On the 4th, to his other symptoms became superadded vomiting of matters similar to those voided. On the 5th, the frequency with which he was moved was still greater than before ; the clots passed were of considerable size ; vomiting was still more urgent ; exhaustion had set in, and on the 6th he died.

In the *post-mortem* examination it was recorded that the body was covered with fat, the liver large, but showing no other signs of disease; the large intestine ulcerated in longitudinal oblong patches along its interior, its surface of a dark bluish colour.

There is, perhaps, no disease in the treatment of which absolute rest is more necessary than it is in dysentery, and certainly there is none in which removal by such means as in India are commonly employed for transport of the sick is so likely to be injurious. This is so evident when we consider the nature of the tissues involved that I need not in this place further dwell upon it than to remark that the discomfort, jolting, and necessary exposure, not alone on field service, but on an ordinary march, act most injuriously upon persons affected with this disease; and that, however great may be the benefit obtained in many cases of disease from rapid change and the jactitation inseparable from travelling in that country, it is essential that the patient labouring under dysentery be not removed until the active stage of the malady has subsided. In those cases where the affection has become chronic the conditions are altogether different. The wonderful effect for good exerted in them by removal, more especially if it be to sea, is well known to all officers of experience in the treatment of tropical diseases.

I have already alluded to the prevalence, in the lower parts of Bengal, of the hæmorrhagic form of this affection. In the majority of stations further inland, where the soil is more arid and the atmosphere less humid, the inflammatory is the more common; but persons debilitated by fever, insufficient food, or by more length of Indian service, not unfrequently become the subjects of the former even there. It has, moreover, been found that the rate of mortality from dysentery has always hitherto been greatest during periods when fevers prevailed in an endemic form.

The experience of 1857-8 induces me to believe that a soldier attacked with severe dysentery on the march must almost to a certainty die from the disease unless it be practicable to at once give him the advantage of being left in a stationary hospital. Men affected with mere trivial attacks of diarrhœa, if arising from irritation of the intestinal canal, often have that malady converted first into inflammatory dysentery, and then into hæmorrhagic, by the continued jolting in a dooly on successive long marches; added to which the exposure to chills, to which they are subject when obliged to attend to the calls of the disease during the night, and in the cold morning air while on the march, are of themselves most injurious.

I have already given cases in illustration of the two forms of dysentery most frequently met with in India. In both extensive disorganization of the large intestines was present; and indeed it is difficult to believe in the occurrence of a case of dysentery in which there is not destruction of tissue to some extent at least. That such are not altogether wanting, however, is indicated in that which follows, its subject having, no doubt, by the exposure and fatigues he had undergone, been reduced to a condition of body in which the tone of his tissues and functions generally were much lowered.

Private Patrick Drennan, 10th Regiment, aged thirty-two years; thirteen years in India; admitted, August 22, 1857; died, 27th; under treatment five days. Came in from Jugdespore, where he had much exposure, fatigue, and wet. Six days previous was seized with severe purging of blood, after having been wet all night. Had to march every day, and on arriving at Dinapore was much exhausted; skin clammy and cold; pulse feeble and soft; purged every few minutes, the blood trickling away as he went from bed to stool. Quinine, three grains, and opium, one grain, every hour; chloroform to abdomen. The flux continuing, he, on the night of the 24th, had gallic acid and quinine, each five grains, opium two grains, every hour; turpentine fomentations and turpentine enemata. These moderated the purging, but he has prolapsus ani from straining. He had dysentery on two former occasions, first in 1846 and in 1854, but in neither so severely as now. On the morning of the 26th improvement had taken place; he felt more comfortable, and was somewhat less often purged; hæmorrhage ceasing. Continue medicines. It would appear that the improvement was but temporary. The flux continued unchecked by the use of medicine; on that night the frequency with which he was purged increased; the evacuations were pure blood. On the 27th there was very copious discharge of fluid blood, and he rapidly sank and died.

The *post-mortem* appearances in this case were :—Liver healthy; bowels pale and bloodless; colon tinged internally with partially coagulated blood.

The notes of this case distinctly state that examination failed to detect the presence of ulcers within the colon, or other disorganization of the intestine. We are therefore forced to believe that, however rare such instances may be, yet that under certain conditions fatal hæmorrhage may occur by exosmosis of blood through the mucous membrane, and without the presence of ulceration.

Subsequent experience induces me to believe that in cases not only of inflammatory dysentery, but in those of the hæmorrhagic type of the disease, enemata of hot water repeatedly administered are not only highly to be recommended as means of treatment, but that they afford an amount of relief to the patient that by no other means can be obtained. I do not mean by this the repeated introduction of long enema tubes, such as were some years ago in common use in India, but the administration of lavements in the ordinary manner. Nor can I too strongly urge the great benefit and relief derivable from the very simple means of permitting patients affected with dysentery to sit upon commodes containing hot water. The vapour soothes the pain of straining in a manner that nothing else does, and thus, no doubt, becomes a powerful means of cure. One other remark on treatment I would here make. It is to recommend in those terrible cases of hæmorrhagic dysentery, such as I have described, that, where gallic acid fails to check the flux, a solution of alum with diluted sulphuric acid added, or of acetate of lead with acetic acid, should be tried. But let us hope that, with improved sanitary conditions among our troops in India, such forms of disease as have been just described shall for the future only occur in rare and exceptional circumstances.

Some years ago a translation of a book by Dr. Bleeker, of Batavia, appeared in the Indian "Annals of Medicine," and attracted much attention. According to that author the early stage of hæmorrhagic or, as he called it, malarious dysentery, consisted in hyperæmia and retention of blood in the mucous and submucous tissues, indicated in the first instance by mucous and muco-sanguineous evacuations; then by the deposit of exudation beneath and in the mucous membrane of the colon, indicated by hæmorrhagic or chocolate-coloured evacuations.

According to Morehead, the most striking effects in restraining the discharge of hæmorrhagic dysentery were obtained from the practice of Dr. Leith. This consisted in administering gallic acid in doses of eight grains, with a couple of drachms of tincture of catechu every hour and a half, port wine being at the same time given freely. This plan was, with many others, tried in the 10th Regiment, but, unhappily, without the success attributed to it by the author named. Quinine is frequently used, and it is stated with considerable success, in the treatment of the hæmorrhagic form of dysentery, more especially in Batavia, Rangoon, and in fact wherever in India malarious influences prevail with great intensity.

In the early part of these remarks, I mention the circumstance that the disease in the 10th Regiment prevailed to the most fatal extent during seasons when fevers affected the men to an unusual extent, and also when the soldiers were subjected to great atmospherical change, and debilitated by severe duty and exposure. I cannot, therefore, better conclude this portion of the subject than by quoting the statement of two eminent authorities, whose expressed opinions are fully corroborated by my own personal observations. Dr. Watson, in his work "On Practice of Physic," states "that whatever gorges the splenic vein gorges its tutelary, the inferior mesenteric, which carries the blood from the colon and rectum; before such congestion of the mucous membrane, inflammation is engrafted, and in this way (indirectly) dysentery may be said to result from marsh effluvia. Ague is au effect of malaria, and dysentery is sometimes a sequel of ague. In precisely the same way dysentery is apt to supervene in hot climates upon hepatic congestion and disease."

Annesley looks upon dysentery as often caused by exposure to night air, and believes it to prevail most at stations characterised by great heat and moisture during the day, and cold dews at night.

When dysentery passes into the chronic form, not only is the health of the person so affected seriously jeopardised, and recovery always distant and uncertain, but accession of the symptoms in an active form is at all times liable to occur from exposure, whether by accident or carelessness to the ordinary causes of intestinal disorders. Patients thus affected are not now ever retained in India, but are sent either to England or to the continent of Europe, with the view of restoration to health. Of the nature of attacks from which men and officers thus sent home are liable to suffer even a considerable time after leaving India, the following case is a fair illustration, and considering the importance of my present subject to army medical officers, I trust I may record it, although not strictly within the sphere indicated in the title of these papers.

W. C. L. had been in England a year, having been invalided from India in consequence of dysentery. Had suffered on several occasions since his return to this country from accessions of that disease, and in the early part of Nov., 1859, had an attack of greater severity than usual. He was then quartered with his regiment at Newbridge, and having been recommended to proceed to his friends at Brighton, left Dublin by one of the Irish steamers. The weather he experienced on the passage was boisterous, and the consequence was that his condition became so alarming, that on the arrival of the vessel at Plymouth, he had immediately to be landed. This occurred on 20th Dec. following, at which time his condition was thus described :—He was suffering severely from abdominal pains ; the limbs and body were cold ; he had constant retching ; was purged every ten minutes or so, passing small quantities of clear jelly-like matter, slightly tinged with blood ; straining was very severe. He immediately on being seen had chloroform, ♏ x. in a little soda-water ; a sinapism was applied to the abdomen. An enema, consisting of tinct. opii, ʒss. in one ounce of starch was administered as soon as possible, and he was directed to take every second hour a pill composed of pulv. Jacobi, grs. ij. ; opii, gr. ss. ; pulv. ver. capsici, gr. ss. ; kino, gr. i.

He obtained some degree of relief in the course of the night, and the report of his state on the 21st mentioned that he was not worse than on the previous evening. The vomiting had been checked, purging was attended by less suffering, the evacuations were less slimy than they had been, but had the characteristic dysenteric odour, the tongue was thickly coated with grey fur. He was now ordered in addition to the former pills, which were to be continued, those composed as follows—one every six hours—namely : Pil. hyd. et pulv. Jacobi, aa gr. i. ; extracti gentianæ, gr. ij. The only nourishment he was allowed was milk. On the evening of the 22nd, at his urgent request, he was permitted to have a little coffee. On the 23rd he was very weak, but he described his own sensations as being decidedly improved. He had slept several hours at intervals, and the abdominal pain, which for some time had continued to recur in paroxyms, was now much diminished. The medicines were steadily continued.

On the evening of the 25th he vomited a little liquid, which, although not coloured by bile, was described as being bitter to the taste. During the early part of that day he had taken more fluid than usual. Was purged about every second hour ; the evacuations liquid, fœcal, but containing some streaks of blood. The bladder sympathised with the irritation in the rectum. Occasional paroxysms of severe pain recurred in the abdomen. The tongue continued much coated, but the tip showed some slight tendency to clean. Pulse 88, of moderate strength. The treatment to be strictly continued.

On the morning of the 26th he was much in the same condition. He had been moved every two hours ; the character of the evacuations as on the previous evening. In addition to the abdominal pain, which still occurred in paroxyms, he now complained much of severe spasms affecting the lower jaw and neck. He was very weak. Tongue as on the former day, and yet he expressed himself as conscious of his own sensations being still further improved. He was now directed to take one of each of the pills already ordered every alternate two hours.

On the evening of that day the tongue had begun to assume a more distinctly moist appearance than it had hitherto presented. The purging and other symptoms were as last described. The treatment was therefore persisted in.

On the morning of the 27th, the improvement in the state of the tongue had not advanced. Thirst, which had from the time when he was first seen been urgent, was now less so. The urine was high coloured and scanty. Considerable tenderness existed over the region of the bladder. He had slept tolerably well during the night, and purging was somewhat less frequent than it had been. Evacuations had become still more fœcal than they had been, and the mucus in them had decreased in quantity. There was no general tenderness of the abdomen, nor did that feeling of *bogginess* exist, which, to the experienced touch, is perceptible in advanced stages of this disease. The paroxysms of sickness and pain, although not entirely ceased, had become much less severe, and the spasm affecting the muscles of the jaw and neck had altogether ceased. The pulse continued at 88, with moderate power. The spirits were improving, as were also the patient's sensations as to his own condition. Medicines continued.

On the morning of the 28th, a very distinct improvement was recorded to have taken place. The tongue was cleaning, and was moist. The evacuations were less frequent, were voided with less suffering than previously, and were still more distinctly fœcal. The irritability of the bladder had also diminished. The medicines still to be continued.

In the evening of that day he was found to have been more frequently purged, although without pain. The evacuations were fœeal, but very offensive. He was directed to omit the use of his former medicine, and to substitute the following, namely—pulv. catechu., gr. ij.; opii gr. ss.; pulv. Jacobi, gr. i.; ex. gent., gr. ss., in pill; and a mixture composed of æth. chloric. m. xv.; spt. ammon. aromat., m. xv.; in ordinary chalk mixture flavoured with syrup of orange peel. One of these pills and a dose of the mixture were directed to be taken after each evacuation.

The morning report of the 29th states that the diarrhœa had been checked, although the character of the evacuations continued much what they were on the previous day. The irritability of the bladder had also diminished, but the spasms in the neck (trismus) had become more severe than they had been since their first occurrence.

The medicines last prescribed were omitted, and he reverted to the use of the first ordered forms of pills.

During the 30th, the state of the bowels had slightly improved. The trismus had given way. The evacuations were less frequent, but still fœcal. The medicine was continued.

On the morning of the 31st he was very much better. He had enjoyed a good night, having only been moved four times. The evacuations unchanged in character, save that they contained a little mucus. Throughout that day the bowels continued to be moved about every second hour; the evacuations at times tinged slightly with blood, but in other respects unaltered in character. The straining and abdominal pain were both less severe than they had been, but there was considerable irritability of the bladder.

During the forenoon of 1st January, 1860, the diarrhœa

had increased, in so far as the amount voided was concerned, although not in the frequency of the evacuations. The proportion of blood voided with them had increased, but portions of the evacuations were semi-consistent and fœcal. The trismus was less urgent than it had been, but a considerable degree of *rawness* was complained of along the course of the transverse colon. A cataplasm, with some mustard, was applied; the pills were omitted, the mixture continued, and he was directed to take every three hours one of the second description of pills that had been ordered, namely, those containing ½ grain of opium, catechu, grs. ii., and capsicum, gr. i.

On the evening of the 2nd an improvement in his condition was again reported; the tongue was cleaning and moist. He had not been much moved during the night; there was no thirst; trismus was less urgent; pulse 80, soft; and he for the first time relished a small piece of toast with tea. He was directed to continue the pills last ordered, and the mixture.

The notes of the case state that from this time to the morning of the 6th he continued as above described; the frequency of his evacuations gradually decreased, the tongue became cleaner, he felt a little appetite, and in all respects progressed favourably. On that date, however, a slight accession of diarrhœa took place. The evacuations were of a dark clay colour, and yeasty in appearance, unmixed with blood, but offensive. A dose of fifteen grains of confection of senna, fifteen of carbonate of magnesia, with tincture of ginger and aromatic spirit of ammonia, was administered, and with much benefit.

On the morning of the 7th, the notes of the case recorded that the evacuations had become more natural in character, and had diminished in frequency. The pills of the 1st were therefore re-ordered. From that date he progressed so favourably that on the 8th the astringent mixture was omitted. On the morning of the 9th he stated that he had only been moved at midnight and again at eight a.m. The evacuations were liquid, fœcal; sensations natural, and tongue clean. He now expressed himself as very hungry. He was therefore considered to be convalescent. The pills were ordered to be continued as before. The diet was and had been entirely farinaceous.

From the above date improvement was progressive, and on the 30th he proceeded to his relatives at Brighton.

This case I consider illustrative of the nature of attacks to which, for a considerable time after their return to Britain, persons who have suffered from the acute form of the disease in India, are liable. It is, moreover, valuable as illustrating the various phases assumed by such attacks, and, I think, of the means by which these are to be best combated.

Hepatitis.

Soldiers in India suffer more largely from hepatic inflammation than those quartered in other tropical regions, whether in China or the West Indies. This class of diseases vary much in their rate of prevalence at different stations in that country, and, as might be anticipated, are much affected by seasons; thus there exists a general impression in India, the truth or otherwise of which can of course be readily tested by statistics, that not only is the rate of prevalence of liver disease different in the different Presidencies, but that similar variety takes place in the frequency of abscess in that viscus, and in its depth, and even in the circumstance of whether suppuration occurs in one large cyst or in several small ones. These subjects are ably discussed by Geddes and Annesley.

Various explanations have been given in regard to this difference in the rate of occurrence of the disease under apparently similar circumstances. Hunter* mentioned the fact in 1808, but attempted no explanation of it. Davy,† more recently, in alluding to it, expresses an opinion that the difference depends, in some measure at

* Diseases of the Army, page 304.
† *Ibid*, page 130.

least, on the amount of out-door exercise in which the climate permits a soldier to indulge, the prevalence being greatest where the men are least out of doors. Other causes, according to him, include the kind of diet and drink used, confinement in ill-ventilated rooms, continued high temperature, and elevation of the locality above sea level. My own experience does not enable me to express a decided opinion regarding the influence exerted by these circumstances, but I enumerate them here as deserving further attention.

With regard to the season during which hepatitis principally attacks our soldiers in India, I find that of 225 cases of which I have statistics, there occurred 68 between April and June, 71 from July to September, 50 from October to December, and 36 between January and March. The rainy season is thus shown, as indeed might have been expected, to be that during which the disease prevails most generally; and as indicating the near approximation that exists between the occurrence of "liver" and malarious fever, I observe that while an average of 4·66 cases of that affection are shown to have occurred per 100 strength during the period in question, the proportion of cases of the latter was 4·22. It has, moreover, been observed that the periods of their greatest prevalence were nearly alike, fevers having been most numerous in August and September, and hepatitis in these months and July.

If we consider the meteorological conditions that characterise each of the periods first alluded to, they may be briefly characterised thus:—From April to June the temperature is high, but its variations small; the atmosphere is dry, its degree of saturation at its minimum; from the occurrence of storms the atmosphere was in frequent and rapid movement; electricity in a frequent state of fluctuation, and evaporation at its maximum. From July to September the general average height of the thermometer is somewhat less, but the diurnal variations still very small; humidity is at its maximum, the air seldom disturbed by electric discharges, and evaporation at its minimum. From October till the end of December the temperature undergoes considerable decrease, and the daily variation increases ; the mornings and evenings are cool and bracing, the atmosphere is less saturated, and its capacity for evaporation greater than in the preceding period. In the succeeding three months—namely, from January to March—a gradual increase of temperature takes place, the daily variations diminish, and the dryness of the air still further increases.

With regard to the period of a soldier's residence in which the liability to hepatitis, as well as the rate of mortality by that disease, are greatest, my statistics indicate that in the first year attacks are relatively rare ; but when they do occur, the rate of mortality is very great. From that time to the fourth year the liability to attack fluctuates, but in an increasing ratio, the mortality being small. In the fifth year the proportion of attacks is not very great, but the rate of mortality by them the largest of any period of which I am in possession of statistics. In the sixth year the number of attacks are far more numerous than in any similar period of Indian residence; but the liability to death by these attacks is less than half as great than it is during the first year of residence in India. From the seventh to the ninth year the liability to attack and to death by the disease fluctuates, but with a downward tendency ; both to take a most material rise in the tenth ; the rate of mortality even then, however, is about one-fourth of what it was in the fifth year, and liability to the disease nearly equal to what it was in the sixth. To prosecute this inquiry further is now rendered unnecessary, as soldiers are unlikely to continue with their regiments in India beyond ten years.

That this form of disease may, and often does, occur from long-continued exposure to what is called "malaria," and without the intervention of any definite *exciting* cause, is now pretty generally allowed. It is also understood among army surgeons that repeated attacks of intermittent fever sooner or later end in organic disease of the liver, and that, therefore, removal of the affected person from the local influenees to which he owed the primary symptoms should take place before the tendeney to fever has become habitual. In many cases, removal to the hills will be sufficient; but in others, departure from India is alone effectnal. I am aware that the dependenee of the disease upon this cause is doubted by Dr. Budd* who, states that he had, when visiting physician to the *Dreadnought*, continually to treat patients arriving from the coast of Afriea in the most deplorable state from fever caught on the West Coast of Africa, but in none of whom did hepatie abseess exist. This fact, however, seems to me to indieate what has already been stated in regard to the varying liability of persons to the disease aecording to loeality. Persons who have seen fever of whatever type on the Afriean Coast and in India are aware of differences in their respective phenomena, while those of considerable Indian experience will, I think, agree with me in the belief that there suppuration of the liver is one of the many effeets of malarial poisoning. Indeed, Dr. Budd, in the very next page after that to which referenee has been made, alludes to such differenees, and also to the possibility of the condition existing in India, although not elsewhere observed.

Aceording to my observations, hepatitis oeeurs in greatest proportion among soldiers, next among offieers. There is among women about one ease of the disease per 100 persons for every four that oeeur among men; and among children, although eases do oecur, they are of great rarity. How far the habits of the three first classes affeet their liability to this disease is a question that early attraets the attention of medical officers; and notwithstanding that differences of opinion in regard to it do exist, I may briefly notiee a few of the habits which distinguish them in the mass. The soldier, heedless of exposure to the weather, whether there be fierce sunshine, rain, or wind, seeks in

* On the Liver, page 95.

"drink" temporary relief from the effects of his recklessness. The balance of circulation is thus upset, and the liver suffers. Officers, as a rule, drink less spirits but considerably more beer than soldiers; they are not, as a class, so reckless as the men in regard to exposure and other irregularities; and women are not only far more temperate, but expose themselves in an infinitesimal degree to the elements or to other causes of exhaustion.

It is doubtless more than probable that the great majority of cases of hepatitis in both soldiers and officers owe their cause to the circumstances just noted. It is by no means the case, however, either that exposure and indulgence will necessarily induce the disease, or that none except the drunken and the indiscreet become affected with the disease. Spirits may, and probably do, induce the adhesive form of inflammation or cirrhosis, but not the suppurative form, such as we are now considering. This has been observed to occur in England* as well as in India; but as the affection chiefly concerns the army medical officer as being a secondary condition found in old soldiers whose service is nearly expired, and who probably would have been discharged had they survived, I need not further allude to it.

In former days, many cases of hepatitis doubtless were produced by the system then in force of allowing soldiers to drink undiluted spirits at the regimental canteen before their dinner, which meal is usually served up at one o'clock. Not only this disease, but others, more especially heat-apoplexy, were attributed to this cause; and the circumstance led to the objectionable practice being abandoned. No doubt many cases of the disease are still directly induced by excesses at the present date, but I would protest against the theory often so plausibly adduced by authors "who live at home at ease," that the malady, and in fact, all others by which mortality in India is increased to a ratio so far beyond that of Britain

* Budd "On the Liver," page 98.

is always attributable to excesses and indiscretions on the part of the sufferers, and not to the climatorial influences of that country. There doubtless are instances as there are in England and elsewhere of individuals by their own indiscretion bringing disease and death upon themselves ; and there may even be a somewhat larger proportion who do so in India than at home. To assert, however, dogmatically, as is sometimes done, that such is the general condition of matters in India is not only in itself erroneous but cruelly unjust to our countrymen, who are defending our national interests in that country.

As we have already seen, children are not altogether exempt from the disease ; the circumstance, moreover, has often been noted that the lower animals brought to Bengal from the neighbouring hills and from Europe, manifest an equal liability to the affection as the human species. Dr. Hooker mentions this with reference to the yâk from Thibet, and there are few officers who have been accustomed to have home-bred dogs there that have not had to treat them for as grievous attacks of "liver" as they may have experienced in their own persons. These are notorious facts in India ; but I mention them here in the hope of being instrumental in removing opinions of an opposite tendency that exist among the inexperienced.

In my remarks on dysentery, I alluded to the value that would accrue, not only to individuals, but to the service, had we the power to state with tolerable precision, whether a particular person was, from his temperament and other characteristics, likely to be attacked by endemic tropical disease, than another of different conditions. This has a peculiar application to Hepatitis, which is believed to prevail in India to an extent equal in proportion to that of pulmonary consumption in Britain. Persons of bilious temperament are usually believed to be most liable to this disease ; but I have reason to doubt the conclusion, and would commend the inquiry to the attention of those who alone can furnish statistics by which it may ultimately be determined. Sir George Ballingall, when serving in the Madras Presidency many years ago, instituted statistics of this nature, but unfortunately they do not appear to have been kept up.

The tendency of inflammation of substance of the liver to run on to suppuration, and the rapidity with which in many cases it does so are both well known to many surgeons in India. They also know that it is not always in cases were the sufferer complains of the greatest pain that this unfortunate occurrence is really most to be dreaded, but that it is so in those where dull, heavy pain deeply seated is experienced, and where pyrexia and other constitutional symptoms are of inconsiderable severity; and this is especially the case in persons whose residence in the country has extended over a few years. Other cases occur in which suppuration takes place absolutely without the presence of any symptoms, such as might be supposed to indicate the mischief in progress. An example of this will be seen presently in the case of Featherstone; many similar will doubtless present themselves to medical officers with regiments in India, amply confirming the observations on the subject by Andral, Abercrombie, and other writers on hepatic disease. Nor is it necessary that this condition be accompanied by dysentery. It may occur in the absence altogether of that complication. When suppuration occurs in the form of one large abscess, the patient seldom survives any considerable length of time unless, as in some rare instances, the contents of the abscess are evacuated by artificial opening, or discharge themselves by the lungs, or intestines. Even in such cases danger is great that death may occur while the process of evacuation is going on; either by exhaustion; by blood poisoning; by peritonitis or suffocation; yet, rare as recoveries are from such conditions, they are sufficiently frequent to justify a hope that, under certain circumstances, this happy result may happen. Perhaps, indeed, recovery in cases such as these, rare, although it be in India, occurs in that country more frequently than it does in other tropical stations; at all events, there is scarcely a hot season in which some case of internal evacuation of a hepatic abscess, terminating in recovery of the, patient does not present itself, and every now and then, also, one in which a similar result followed the operation of paracentisis. I had an opportunity, on various occasions while superintending invaliding at Calcutta, from 1862 to 1867, to observe such instances, and yet Dr. Davy * whose experience in the colonies was very extensive, states that he has never known recovery take place from an abscess of the liver, that either broke internally or was opened by the surgeon.

One attack of the disease is very often, but by no means invariably followed by another, if the person attacked remains continuously in India, or returns to the country after short absence. As a rule, however, soldiers who are invalided to England on account of "liver" are not again efficient if sent back to that country; the exceptions alluded to being chiefly among officers and other members of the better classes, whose education and circumstances enable them to avoid or mitigate the causes to which a former attack may have been attributable. In many of the persons who thus, on their return to India, become again the subjects of hepatitis, they begin early in the hot season to experience indisposition; the symptoms, however, may not be of a nature to indicate the extent of visceral disorganization that is actually in progress, although the medical officer does not fail to observe the change in colour and expression of countenance that gradually take place, the so-called "dyspepsia" of which the patient complains, and finally the hectic flush and diarrhœa that form the alarming indications of the mischief that has been done.

Chronic hepatitis, on the other hand, prevails to a great extent during the cold season; attacks of this form of the disease are also observed to be induced by sudden or great alternations of temperature, by the jolting inci-

---

* Diseases of the Army, page 156.

dental to long journeys, and by the fact of removal to the climate of the Hills. One indication obtained from these facts to which I may now allude, is the propriety of sending all invalids suffering from the affection by long sea journey to England instead of *viâ* Overland. Change to the Hills has not been shown by experience to benefit, as a rule, persons suffering from this affection, and indeed there is reason to believe that attacks are not seldom induced by it.

Many cases of deranged function of the viscus itself, and many of so-called dyspepsia or indigestion in persons who have spent a number of years in India, date their commencement from an attack of hepatitis ; others are but manifestations of chronic hyperæmia of the viscus, ending it may be, sooner or later, in suppuration. It is, therefore, unadvisable to retain in India a soldier or officer who manifests either of the above "functional derangements." Their true nature often reveals itself in an attack of dysentery or diarrhœa ; and, after death, a succession of small abscesses deep in the liver are discovered. Similar symptoms in other cases are probably the result of induration of the organ, to which allusion has already been made, while cases are by no means rare in which functional disorder confined to the duodenum simulate liver disease so exactly, that correct diagnosis is by no means easy.

Cases are not rare among soldiers and officers in India where the secretion of bile is increased, giving rise to vomiting and to discharge of that liquid by the bowels. Attacks of this nature may, or may not, be attended by symptoms of inflammation, or congestion of the liver ; they are generally acompanied by considerable constitutional disturbance ; are present among new arrivals, but also occur among those who have been some time in the country. In the latter, such an attack often accompanies malarious fever, and should be held as indicating liability to actual hepatic disease, and the necessity of removal of the person suffering to a temperate climate.

Cases also occur in which the passage of one or more gall-stones produces symptoms so similar to those of actual hepatic inflammation as to be distinguished from it with difficulty, if at all. Army surgeons can afford to relate their difficulties, as well as their successes.

I would in this place give an account of two cases in which openings were made into an abscess of the liver. In both the result was unfortunate, yet not under such circumstances as to discourage a medical officer, even had other cases of success, after a similar operation, not been on record. Puncturing, or otherwise opening an abscess in this organ, however, is a very different matter from the system of one time in use of *exploring* the viscus, a system that, fortunately for the good of the sick soldier, has been all but abandoned in India. Prior to 1841, it was carried to excess for a short time, and when, during the three years succeeding, I served in that country in the *Buffs*, I had several opportunities of observing marks of the exploring needle in livers that presented no other morbid appearance.

With regard to the operation of opening abscesses of the viscus, Waring gives statistics according to which it would appear that, in 81 cases of hepatic abscess opened in India, there were 15 survivors, and 66 deaths ; but I must refer the reader who desires complete details on the subject to French's Clinical Treatise.

Featherstone, 10th Foot, aged twenty-nine, eleven years in the service, arrived in India late in 1842 ; shortly after landing suffered from dysentery, from which his recovery was incomplete, inasmuch that he had occasional recurrences of the disease from that time to 1845. During that and the following year he accompanied his regiment on service against the Sikhs, being, at Sobraon, shot in the leg and severely wounded by a sabre cut in the head, he killing his adversary as he fell. From these wounds, however, he recovered, and for the two following years, during which he was present with his regiment at Meerut, retained good health, and was free from any return of his dysentery.

In 1848, the regiment being quartered in the citadel of Lahore, he for the first time experienced symptoms of "liver disease," and in that year sustained an attack of the disease, on account of which he was three months under treatment. On being discharged from hospital, he accompanied the regiment to Mooltan, and during the whole of the campaign against that fortress enjoyed good health; he subsequently accompanied the corps to Ferozepore, and in 1850 to Wuzzeerabad. Towards the latter end of that year he suffered at that station from an attack of ague; in October, 1851, had a return of the disease, and in the succeeding month was under treatment for dysentery, but without any indication of liver disease.

On the 9th of February, 1851, the appearance of this man was such that Dr. Inglis, C.B., at that time in the 10th, remarked it during his ordinary inspection of barracks, and directed him to be sent to hospital. On being questioned there, he complained of a dull sense of weight and uneasiness in the region of the liver, and in the back; extending to the shoulder, increased on pressure, and attended by an irritable condition of the stomach; pulse was rapid, skin hot and dry.

On the 16th of that month, there was considerable bulging of the hepatic region, with a remote indication from elasticity, &c., of the formation of pus having taken place in the liver; he complained of constant pain in the affected side; the countenance was pallid, approaching yellow; appetite defective; strength prostrate; no febrile excitement. From this time he continued to manifest distinct symptoms of abscess in the liver, and the upper part of the right lobe was diagnosed as being its site.

On the 13th, a trocar and canula were pushed downwards into the projecting tumour from immediately below the false ribs; on withdrawing the canula, a spout of matter followed, and two pints of matter were in this way evacuated. A sense of relief was for a short time experienced, but he shortly afterwards complained of some degree of oppression in the right side of the chest, although a bandage had been applied in the ordinary way after the operation.

On the night of the 14th, he became restless; pain occurred in the abdomen; it soon became evident that the man was sinking, and during the night of the 15th he died.

Post-mortem appearances.—Although the canula had been retained in the wound, no attempt had been made at reparative action; the external opening communicated with a very large sac which occupied the whole of the right lobe of the liver, and an opening was discovered to have taken place spontaneously into the corresponding pleura.

The above case illustrates what has already been stated in regard to the insidious manner in which suppuration sometimes occurs, and as illustrating the ordinary progress of an unsuccessful case of the disease in question.

Murray, 10th Foot, admitted into hospital at Wuzzeerabad, 16th March, 1852, aged at the time thirty-two. He complained of pain around the umbilicus, which had come on without any apparent cause two days previous, and continued to increase in severity; his calls to stool were frequent, evacuations scanty and containing much blood and slime. Leeches were applied, calomel and opium administered, followed by a dose of castor-oil.

On the 18th, was reported as nearly free from pain, but passed a restless night; complained of thirst, and his pulse was somewhat excited; bowels only moved twice.

19th.—An attack of purging came on at three a.m., but was relieved by appropriate remedies; pain increased in the region of the stomach, and great irritability of that organ came on, so that for several days from this time the only medicines that could be administered consisted of effervescent draughts, a blister being applied externally.

On the 27th, slight tympanitis of the abdomen existed, but in other respects his symptoms appeared somewhat decreased in severity.

30th.—The report of his case records that during the previous three days he had a succession of chills, and that now distinct enlargement of the liver can be felt, and also indistinct signs of suppuration of that viscus detected.

About this time he stated that, shortly before his admission into hospital, he had, while in the act of lifting a heavy weight, tripped his foot, and suddenly felt as if something had given way in his middle ; and he dated his illness from that accident.

No material change in his condition is recorded till the 1st of April, on which date the report of his case states that he was again seized with shivering, succeeded by a hot and a sweating stage ; the tumour in the epigastrium had become more distinct than it had been, and nocturnal perspirations had set in.

On the morning of the 3rd, he had a very severe attack of shivering, and the tumefaction over the liver became much increased, filling up the entire space from the umbilicus to the ribs. The patient experienced no difficulty in lying upon either side. An operation having been determined upon, an oblique incision was made downwards and outwards from about an inch below the cartilage of the false ribs ; the rectus muscle was divided, and a trocar and canula pushed upwards and inwards through the tumour the whole length of the tube. Forty ounces of pus, interspersed with clear glairy-looking matter, were at once evacuated, with the usual precautions, the canula being secured in the wound.

On the 4th, nine ounces of pus were in the morning evacuated, and six more in the evening, the dressings being soaked with bile and coloured yellow. He expressed himself as much relieved, and was in good spirits. An anodyne draught was administered, and during the succeeding night he had tolerable sleep.

On the 5th, about an ounce of blood-coloured matter was evacuated, and in the course of that day, while he was in the act of changing his position, the canula slipped from the wound ; it was, however, replaced, and for the time no evil consequences appeared to result.

On the 6th, he was reported to have had a good night, to have slept tolerably well ; two ounces more of matter were evacuated from the wound. The pulse was soft and of natural frequency; tongue clean. He was in good spirits, and expressed himself as feeling stronger.

According to the report of the 8th, he had been purged four times during the previous night. He had slept well for four hours, but unfortunately during that time turned awkwardly in bed, and instantly awoke, feeling that he had injured himself in the vicinity of the wound.

At the morning visit on the 9th, his features were observed to be somewhat sunken, but no other unfavourable indication for a time presented itself. The pulse was moderate; skin moist. About noon, unequivocal symptoms of peritonitis set in, and from that moment the case was considered as beyond hope; the new disease progressed rapidly, notwithstanding the use of as active remedies as the case admitted of. He gradually became more and more weak, abdominal pain ceased, and on the 14th, at five p.m., he expired.

Post-mortem appearances, seven hours after death.—Slight adhesions existed around the opening into the liver, the external orifice of that in the organ itself being dark in colour, and presenting a semi-gangrenous appearance; the entire lower aspect of the right lobe formed but a sac of an abscess, the cavity of which was sufficiently large to admit the fist. Its inner surface was lined with a layer of what seemed to be lymph, over which was a coating of dark offensive matter. No opening into the abdomen through the adhesions could be discovered, but the whole of that membrane was in a state of inflammation. The intestines were glued together in many places, and in the right hypochondrium suppuration had occurred in some of the glands. The other organs were not examined.

Jaundice.

Although the occurrence of jaundice among troops in India is by no means frequent, a considerable number of cases of the disease appear from time to time. In some cases, it occurs during attacks of acute hepatitis; more frequently it attends chronic attacks of the disease, while in others it presents itself unaccompanied by symptoms of either, although doubtless there exists in all a certain amount of deranged nutrition of the liver, of which the jaundice itself is a more attendant condition.

In a considerable number of cases of malarious fevers, jaundice exists as a complication of the general disease, and in a few the discolouration of the surface and conjunctiva is so great, while the period of evident pyrexia lasts, that persons so affected manifest symptoms approaching more or less closely those of yellow fever in the West Indies. This may be the case with, or in the absence of, symptoms of vascular engorgement of the liver.

It is by no means an easy matter in India, any more than it is at home, to form a correct opinion as to the precise condition upon which jaundice depends, or, in other words, its proximate cause—that is, whether it arises from suppression or retention and re-absorption of bile, as enumerated in the ordinary manuals. When I was surgeon of a regiment there, the method of Dr. Harley to distinguish these classes of cases was not known, at any rate by me, and I would here note them for the benefit of my successors. Jaundice from suppression, according to him,* is distinguished by the circumstance that only those products which exist preserved in the blood accumulate in the circulation, whereas in that from retention or obstruction, the products that are manufactured in the liver, equally with those preserved in the blood, find their way back to the circulation.

Considering the physiology of biliary secretion, and knowing the pernicious results that arise when the eliminating and transforming operations exerted by the liver upon the blood are ineffectually performed, it becomes a matter of surprise how little constitutional derangement attends the vast majority of cases of jaundice met with in

* Aitkin's Science and Practice of Medicine, p. 952. Also, Tanner, p. 153.

India; slight indisposition, with nausea and anorexia, being perhaps the only accompaniments of the malady.

According to the statistics to which I have access, the greatest liability of men to the affection exists during the early years of their residence in India. I observe, however, that after the 10th Regiment had served five years in that country, and after being exposed to a severe outbreak of fever and dysentery, consequent upon occupation of very unsuitable quarters in the citadel of Lahore, a very marked increase took place in the number of cases of jaundice that for some time afterwards occurred. Thus, whereas from the time in question the yearly ratio of cases of the affection was no more than 2·50 per 1,000 mean strength, it subsequently rose to 13·0.

It seems to occur in somewhat larger relative frequency among officers than among men, is less than half as frequent among women as among soldiers, and is somewhat more frequent among children than among females of, and beyond, the age of puberty. Infants at the time of birth, in some instances, are jaundiced.

In some cases, biliary calculi are found in the gall-bladder of persons who have, during life, suffered from jaundice, and died of some other disease. The occurrence of these conditions, however, does not appear to be either constant or necessarily connected with jaundice; for while, on the one hand, that disease is found in persons who are subsequently found free from the presence of hepatitic or biliary calculi, so in others, whose gall-bladder is filled by those masses, no jaundice has been observed.

Fevers.

Fevers as a distinct class of diseases, although numerically more prevalent among troops in India than among those in temperate climates, are far less fatal than under the latter circumstances. Thus, taking the statistics of the 10th Foot for a period of thirteen years, during which time the corps saw a good deal of service, and was stationed at various places in that country, the average annual occurrence of all types of fevers was: among soldiers 1·09 per cent., officers 5·32, women 2·64, and children 4·30; the ratios of mortality to cases being 2·88, 1·41, 4·63, and 11·33 of these classes respectively. From these figures we learn that officers manifest the greatest liability of the classes enumerated to become attacked by fever in some of its forms, but that among them mortality is at its minimum. Children, on the other hand, are comparatively seldom attacked, but when they are so are more liable to death by this cause than either of the three other classes.

Their prevalence is materially influenced by season, geographical position, and by local peculiarities of station; thus, periodic fevers prevail in Bengal in July, August, September—that is, during the three rainy months—and are most severe in the early, and again in the latter, portion of that period. During October and November, the prevalence of fevers, although less, is still considerable, the alternations of temperature between day and night being apparently a powerful cause of the continuance of attacks of intermittents in persons already subjects of that form. Fevers of all kinds still further decrease in frequency, and during January, February, and March are at their minimum. Direct exposure, as during field service, did not appear to produce material increase in the severity of attacks of fever, and under such circumstances the treatment necessary was found to be more simple than in quarters; frequent affusion being the only measure demanded by cases of continued form, while in those of intermittents comparatively small doses of quinine were administered.

Intermittent Fevers.—Statistics indicate that fevers of the intermittent type increase in prevalence according to length of service of soldiers in India; that the distinctions are seldom well marked between the different types of these, and that, although mortality is small indeed by uncomplicated ague, the fact of a person manifesting a liability to recurrences of the disease may be taken as an indication of a tendency to organic affection which may destroy life; and that, therefore, removal out of the country for a longer or shorter period is in such cases absolutely necessary. Of the various classes of persons comprising a regiment, soldiers are the most liable to these affections, next to them the officers, then the soldiers' wives, and, least of all, the children. With regard to mortality, however, no death by intermittent fever except among soldiers and children is recorded as having happened in the 10th Foot during thirteen years it served in the country.

Of 1,672 cases of this form of fever which occurred among soldiers, 1,151 were of the quotidian type, and 521 of the tertian; of 48 among officers, the numbers were respectively 22 and 26; of 130 among women, 109 and 21; and of 74 among children, 65 and 9. Thus, the quotidian was the type most prevalent among soldiers, their wives and children; the tertian was slightly the more common among officers.

On two occasions during the service of the 10th Regiment in India intermittents prevailed as epidemics in the corps. On both of these a heavier rainfall than usual had taken place; no perceptible difference in other meteorological conditions was, however, observable between them and others where the disease did not prevail, and it may be said that the physical causes of the disease were inappreciable.

It should be mentioned that one of the occasions when the disease prevailed in this manner was when the corps occupied temporary barracks at Wuzzeerabad, in the Punjaub, a low lying sandy site, little elevated above the level of the River Chenab, which flowed past it at a distance of about four miles. The layer of surface sand rested upon a bed of stiff clay, containing calcareous nodules; and notwithstanding that, during a great part of the year, the vicinity presented little vegetation, water was at all times to be found in abundance at a depth of not more than six or eight feet.

There are not a few men and officers who have spent many years in India who suffer at irregular and uncertain intervals from attacks of intermittent fever, in whom such attacks would appear to have become habitual, and whose health seems to be temporarily renovated after each. Among those who manifest this liability, an accession may frequently be induced by slight exposure to the sun, night air, a draught of wind, by irregularity in diet, by mental annoyance, or other circumstances that do not affect the robust.

An explanation of such peculiarity is among the difficulties which beset the medical officer in that country. Perhaps we may assume that the particular influence upon which the phenomena of ague depend being imbibed into the system of an individual, it there undergoes a series of changes, and produces particular trains of symptoms according to the degree of *impressionability* of the individual to it; thus, in one person the vital powers may be such that the system eliminates the poison without becoming itself affected thereby. Such cases, however, are of comparatively rare occurrence; but that they do happen is a fact familiar to all of local experience, persons being known to them who for many years have lived in notoriously malarious and aguish localities without being in any way affected thereby. The very much larger and less fortunate classes include, in the first place, persons who, from temporary exposure to concentrated causes of fever, or to protracted exposure to them in a less concentrated form, become the subjects of that fever called respectively remittent, jungle, or marsh fever; and in such cases, provided the patient has sufficient strength to bear him through the original attack, he is left cachectic, anæmic, and greatly debilitated. In the second, we take the case of a strong healthy young man, a keen sportsman, and a person who has for a certain number of years exposed himself in all manner of ways without injury, and whose boast therefore is that "the sun has no power to hurt him." Suddenly, and, it may be, without adequate cause, he is attacked with ague ; he goes through the regular stages of a seizure of this kind, and then returns to his ordinary habits. Soon, however, he is "down" again ; and so on, time after time, until he is reduced to a condition in which removal to a cold climate becomes for him a necessity. Shall we suppose that in such a case the morbific influence has gradually accumulated in the system, defying the vital powers to throw it off, and that, by its continuous presence and accumulation, the functions become impaired and weakened in the manner just described?

It by no means necessarily happens in India that a person undergoes an attack of the more dangerous form of fever before he becomes the subject of ague. The latter form may be the first, or indeed the only one with which during his residence he may be affected ; while, on the other hand, he may have successive attacks of the continued type without being subject to ague. In this respect there is, I think, a great distinction between the manner in which persons stationed respectively in India and on the West Coast of Africa suffer from these affections. On the Coast of Guinea it is, or rather *was*, in 1847-8, observable, that in the case of a white man arriving there for the first time, it mattered not whether he had previously been subject to intermittent fever, he must first undergo an attack of the ordinary endemic fever of the Coast before the ague becomes re-established. So also in the West Indies, the circumstance of a person being the subject of *fever and ague* was at that time considered as indicating his non-liability to the more severe forms, and in that sense the occurrence of the cold stage of intermittent fever was considered a subject of congratulation. I myself have been thus congratulated at Cape Coast Castle. Probably ague was looked upon as a kind of safety-valve to morbid influences that might otherwise induce more serious results.

This type is most common in the months of July, August, and September, or, in other words, during the rainy season. During October and November it also prevails to a considerable extent, but decreases from that time till March, when its prevalence is at its minimum. It does not always happen, however, that an individual obtains benefit by the advent of the cold weather, which serves to restore and "set up" the health of those who, during the long months of intense heat, have been in some measure lowered, but without suffering from actual disease. On the contrary, a temporary increase both in the frequency of the attacks and in their severity often occurs under such circumstances, while some persons who had hitherto remained free from the disease now became attacked.

That attacks of rheumatism often supervene upon fevers in India is well known. In such cases that disease assumes a periodic character; but it has also been observed that a similar tendency occurs in other affections. Various other forms of disease arise as direct effects of exposure to *malaria*, one of the most frequent being enlargement of the spleen, which, as being the most frequent complication of ague, may here be made the subject of a few remarks. Its relative prevalence varies greatly according to the circumstances of particular classes of persons borne upon the rolls of a regiment in India. Thus, I find that among the cases of "fever and ague" in soldiers, already recorded, there were 127 of enlarged spleen, giving a ratio of 7·59 per cent.; among those in officers only one case occurred, or 2·08 per cent.; among all the cases of ague in women there were 7, or 5·39; and among children the spleen was affected in 13, giving the very large proportion of 17·56 per cent.

The very great liability of children to become thus affected is remarked by persons of even moderate experience in India. The little sufferers are immediately recognised by their pallid tumefied face, pale lips, protuberant abdomen, and wasted limbs; those of them whose parents can afford to send them home should be sent to England without delay, and it is to be hoped that with the large extent of accommodation for troops now being prepared in the Hills throughout India, ample means will be provided there for their wives and children affected with this disease and with the many other forms which render a removal from the plains necessary for their recovery. Under existing circumstances, mortality from this cause and its attendant cachexy is among the young very considerable.

On the subject of treatment, I note that while occupied in carrying out some official investigations relative to the comparative success of some reputed remedies, I preserved a record of a considerable number of cases in which quinine in various doses and combinations was administered; and from those records I have prepared the following summary, namely :—

Quotidian Intermittent.—One case in which no medicine was given was discharged recovered in twenty-two days.

One case, treated with 2 grains of quinine three times a day for six days (18 grains), recovered in eight days.

Of four cases treated by 3-grain doses, administered three times a day, one was so during three days, having a total of 27 grains, and recovered in nine days; two during five days, each taking in that time 45 grains; one of the two, being discharged, recovered in five days, the other in six days; and one treated thus for twenty-one days, taking ʒj. grs. 45, was in hospital before recovery eighty-two days. Average, twenty-five days.

Of three treated by 3 grains of quinine and 1 of rhubarb, repeated three times a day, all were so during four days, taking 36 grains. One of these recovered in four days, the other in five, and the third in six. Average, five days.

One case treated by 3-grain doses, repeated four times a day during ten days, taking in that time ʒij. and 6 grains, was at the end of that time discharged recovered.

Three cases were treated by quinine in 5-grain doses, and of them the statistics are as follow, namely :—In one the quantity was administered uncombined three times a day during three days; 45 grains in all were taken, and the patient was discharged recovered in ten days. In two this dose was combined with 1 grain of rhubarb, and repeated three times a day; one patient so treated had ʒj. and 15 grains of the remedy in five days, and was discharged in seven. In one it was similarly administered during four days, 23 grains being taken in all, and the patient discharged in nine days. Average, nine days.

In one case, after this dose and combination had been employed five days, quinine uncombined was given in 3-grain doses thrice during two days, ʒj. grs. 33 being taken in that time, and the patient discharged recovered in nine days.

In another the combination was given three times a day during three days, three grains of uncombined quinine being administered thrice a day during two more; ʒj. grs. 15 taken in all, and the patient discharged recovered in five days. Average, seven days.

One case was treated by 5-grain doses, in combination with 2 of rhubarb, every third hour during two days, and 3 grains of each three times a day during three more; the total quantity taken was ʒj. grs. 15, and the patient was discharged in eleven days.

Five were treated with similar doses of quinine, combined with 3 grains of rhubarb, administered three times a day. In one of these the treatment was continued during three days, the patient taking 45 grains in all, and discharged in four. In one it was continued during four, the quantity taken being ʒj., the patient discharged in sixteen. In two it was continued during seven, the quantity taken being in each case ʒj. grs. 45. One of the patients was discharged in ten, the other in eighteen days; and in the fifth case the treatment was continued during eight days, ʒij. of quinine was taken, and the patient discharged in thirteen days. Average, twelve days.

One patient had 5 grains of quinine and 3 of rhubarb repeated twice in one day, and 2 grains uncombined thrice a day during five; he took in all ʒj. grs. 15 of the remedy, and was discharged in seven days.

Another had a similar combination three times a day

during two days, and then 3 grains of quinine three times during one day; he took in four days 45 grains, and at the end of the time returned to duty.

In two cases the 5-grain dose of quinine was combined with 5 of rhubarb. In one of these this dose was repeated three times during one day, then varied by 1 grain of hyoscyamus being substituted for the latter, and so continued during four days. The patient took in all ʒj. and 15 grains of quinine, and was discharged in thirty-five days. In the other the 5-grain doses of quinine and rhubarb were continued during three days, 3-grain doses of uncombined quinine being given for eight days more, making eleven in all. During that time ʒj. grs. 27 of quinine were taken, the patient being discharged in eleven days. Average of the two, twenty-three days.

Three cases were treated by 10-grain doses of the medicine. Of these, one dose only was given in one case, no further treatment being employed, and the patient discharged recovered in sixteen days. In one the dose was repeated twice a day during two days, 40 grains being taken in that time, and the patient discharged in six days. In another the dose was given once a day during three days, ʒss. of the medicine being taken in all, and the patient discharged in five days.

In three cases one dose of 10 grains was given, and afterwards doses of 5 grains repeated three times a day; one of the patients so treated took ʒj. grs. 14, one ʒj. grs. 35, and the third ʒj. grs. 40 of the remedy, each being discharged in eight days.

Two patients were treated by 10 grains of quinine administered as one dose, the remedy being afterwards administered in doses of 5 grains, with 1 grain of extract of hyoscyamus, repeated three times a day. Of these, one was so treated during four days, ʒj. grs. 10 of quinine being taken, and the patient discharged in six days; the other during five, ʒj. grs. 25 being taken, and the patient discharged in nine days.

One had a single dose of 10 grains, with 3 grains of blue

pill, followed by doses of 3 grains of quinine repeated every four hours. The patient was thus treated three days, took 45 grains of quinine, and was discharged in nine.

One, after having a single dose of 10 grains, was treated by 5-grain doses repeated three times during one day, a similar quantity being given, combined with 3 grains of rhubarb, three times a day during four days. In this case the treatment extended over six days, ʒj. grs. 25 being taken during that time, and the patient discharged in eight.

Another man treated by 10-grain doses had two such, followed thereafter by 3-grain doses three times a day during three days; he took in all 37 grains, and was discharged recovered in six.

Quinine in doses of 30 grains was administered as follows:—In one case only one dose was given; no further treatment was employed, and the patient was discharged in six days. In one the dose was given on two consecutive days; ʒj. was thus taken in all, and the patient discharged in four days. In one, after one dose of 30 grains, the medicine was given in quantities of 5 grains repeated three times a day during two days, and afterwards in doses of 2 grains three times a day during six days; this treatment was employed during eight days, ʒj. grs. 36 of quinine being taken, and the patient discharged in ten days. In another two doses each of 30 grains were administered, followed by a scruple dose twice repeated, and this by 2 grains of quinine, with 5 of rhubarb, repeated three times daily during two days; treatment was thus continued four days, ʒj. grs. 46 of quinine being taken in all, and the patient was discharged recovered in twenty-nine days.

Tertian Fever.—With reference to cases of tertian ague, I obtain the following information, namely:—In one case 2 grains of quinine were given three times a day during four days; 24 grains taken in all, and the patient discharged in eight days. In four cases quinine was administered in 3-grain doses, repeated three times a day. In one of these the treatment was continued four days; 36

grains were taken, and the patient was discharged in nine days. In two it was continued five days, the patient taking 45 grains ; and of these one was discharged at the end of that time, the other being so in seven days. In one the treatment was continued six days ; the patient discharged in fourteen. In one case, after this treatment had been continued seven days, it was modified, 2-grain doses being then given three times a day during six ; this treatment extended over thirteen days ; the patient took in all ʒj. grs. 39, and was discharged in twenty-six days. In another case 3 grains of quinine, combined with 5 of blne pill, were given three times a day during two days, 2 grains of uncombined quinine beiug given three times a day during three more days ; this treatment was continned five days ; 36 grains of quinine given, and the patient at the end of the time discharged to duty. In one case 5-grain doses three times a day were continued duriug ten days, ʒj. grs. 30 being taken in that time, and the patient discharged in eleven days. One was similarly treated during seven days, ʒj. grs. 45 taken in that time, and he discharged in ten ; and one during three days, he taking 45 grains, and being discharged in five. One patient had 5 grains of quinine, with 5 of rhubarb, three times a day during three days ; took 45 grains, and was discharged in four days ; and one who was treated with similar doses of quinine, with two grains of extract of hyoscyamus twice repeated, and then had a single 30-grain dose of quinine all in one day, 45 grains being thus taken, bnt no further treatment used, was discharged in eleven days.

Of two men who had 10-grain doses repeated three times a day, and afterwards by 3-grain doses similarly administered, one had the larger doses during four days, the smaller during two, or six in all ; he took ʒij. grs. 18, and was discharged in sixteen. The other had the larger doses during two days, the smaller in five ; took in all ʒij. grs. 55 in these seven days, and was discharged in twenty-seven.

One had two doses each of 10 grains, succeeded by 2 grains repeated twice a day during two days ; thus he received medicine during three, took in all 28 grains, and was discharged in four; and one who, after one dose of 10 grains, received 5 grains four times in one day, and 2 grains three times a day during eight, was thus under actual treatment nine days, in which he took in all ʒj. grs. 20; he was discharged to duty at the end of that time.

In one case ℈j. of quinine was administered three times a day during two days; ʒij. were taken in all, and the patient discharged in thirteen days.

In one 30 grains were given, and repeated in the same day, after which 5 grains of quinine, with 5 of rhubarb, were given three times daily during three days; the patient was thus four days under treatment, took in all ʒij. grs. 15 of quinine, and was discharged in thirty-four days.

An analysis of these records will not, I fear, tend to increase confidence in the superiority of one method of administering this medicine over another. In conducting my investigations, every endeavour was made to observe similar conditions in the management of all cases which came under observation; various other plans of treatment were moreover observed, of which, although the particulars are unfortunately not now available, I am able to give the conclusions drawn from them at the time. In some cases no other treatment was employed than the exhibition of free purgatives, and keeping the patient several days on spoon diet; and young and robust soldiers so treated while labouring under a first, second, or even third attack of the disease, recovered quite as favourably and rapidly as others did who were treated by the remedies usually recommended. In old cases, however, and in those of patients who were much debilitated, or who laboured under any of the complications of intermittent fever, more especially enlargement of the spleen and cachexy, treatment became a matter of serious difficulty. Quinine in such cases was the remedy most to be confided in, in some dose or other, and combined in the various ways that have been detailed.

But it often happened that, from no evident cause, some

one of the usual remedies given as an anti-periodic would fail, and another succeed. Thus, on the occasions mentioned, the ordinary sulphate of quinine failed to check the accessions, but what was called the amorphous solution speedily had the desired effect; while in others, where first one and then the other of these seemed to have no effect, the employment of arsenical solution, sulphate of biberine, sulphate or carbonate of zinc, were followed by favourable results.

It is useless to warn soldiers against the circumstances that induce intermittent fever. The occurrence of one attack after the committal of an irregularity does not teach them, as a rule, to avoid a similar. Medicine mostly seems to have a partial and uncertain remedial power so long as a person continues under the conditions that in the first instance induced the attack; and therefore the removal of the person to a less malarious district, whether that be in India itself or to England, becomes, in the cases of all who are confirmed subjects of ague, a matter of necessity.

Remittent Fever.

The prevalence of, and mortality by, remittent fever in India appear to be influenced by length of residence in the country, by station, by season, and by the conditions of the different classes of persons borne upon the rolls of a regiment. For my present purpose it will be sufficient to observe that, according to notes in my possession, the occurrence of, and deaths by, this form of disease among soldiers of the 10th Foot during thirteen years the regiment was in India were as follow, namely:—In the first year of its service there the number of cases was 102, of deaths 11; in the second, 26 and 5 respectively; in the third, 14 and none; fourth, 33 and 6; fifth, 11 and 6; sixth, 2 and 1; seventh, 67 and 4; eighth, 12 and 2; ninth, 162 and 4; tenth, 82 and 3; eleventh, 24 and 2;

twelfth, 2 and 1; and thirteenth, 13 and 4. The women rate of mortality, which varied much from year to year, was for the whole period to the cases treated 8·90 per cent. among men, 11·76 among officers, 18·87 among women, and 35·29 among children.

From these and other returns we learn, what has frequently been observed with regard to other diseases, that it is not where the affection is most prevalent numerically that liability to death by it is greatest; neither is the class among which attacks are the most frequent that which furnishes the largest proportion of victims. It is well to observe, however, that, under the term "remittent" fever, two distinct forms of disease are included, both depending upon different conditions, distinguished by different characters, and demanding different methods of management. Of these one, in every respect a marsh fever, similar to the paludal fever of the tropics generally, is termed *jungle* fever; the other, described by Johnson and Martin under the name of ardent remittent fever, occurs in the hottest periods of the year, and for the most part in the more inland districts of India.

The malarial form sometimes prevails as an epidemic at certain stations, and it may be in the recollection of some who read these notes, that so severely were *the Buffs* visited by the disease in this form at Kurnal, that the place was in consequence abandoned. Other places also had a bad reputation on the same account, more especially Dinapore, Berhampore, and Lodianah; the latter station built upon the bank of an old river course. Of late years such recurrences do not take place to anything approaching the extent they formerly did; when cases, however, do occur, they generally happen during the rainy and early part of the cold seasons; and the prevalence of intermittents at the same time is one among several indications that both forms depend upon a common cause.

Of late years such outbreaks may be said to have almost entirely ceased, and a modification has even occurred in the characteristics of the affection. At the time of which

I write various circumstances, now happily removed, combined with such as have just been mentioned to induce the form of disease then observed. Of such were overcrowding and imperfect ventilation; another was the enforced confinement of the men in their barracks, errors then practised on the plea of protecting them from the influences of the sun. Thus, when, on the subjugation of the Punjaub, our troops held occupation of Lahore, both these causes were powerfully in operation, and produced a severe outbreak in the 9th Lancers and 10th Foot. Then also, and for some time subsequent to that date, the practice permitted in some regiments of issuing spirits to soldiers at or shortly after midday, was a further source of the disease. To obtain them the men often rushed from their rooms to the canteen, exposing themselves to the blazing sun, and, in the North-Western Provinces, to the hot winds then prevailing. Having swallowed their allowance of spirits, they returned to their quarters, where, after dinner, they threw themselves on their cots to sleep away the remainder of the day, and in not a few instances to pass into fever, or the more fatal form of disease, heat-apoplexy. All these conditions have now ceased, however, and one of the most apparent among the results of improved sanitation has been the decrease in this disease among our troops.

In cases of malarious forms of the affection, various complications occur which are calculated to mask the real nature of the attack. Thus, dysentery or hepatitis not unfrequently supervene, the disease then assuming many of the ordinary characters of enteric fever of temperate climates. As, however, medical officers who have been some time in India have to learn that visceral lesions are often direct results of malaria, they have not, as a rule, much difficulty in assigning their relative value to these and other complications which appear.

In the treatment of intermittent fever it is almost needless to observe that large doses of calomel, and the free abstraction of blood, were for many years considered in the light of *sheet anchors*, for so the phrase went. Both had even before 1840 fallen considerably into disrepute, and have gradually been quite abandoned; yet it may, as a professional curiosity, be here recorded at what cost to himself the medical officer who first dared to dispute the merits of calomel in this disease declined to follow what then was the *orthodox* plan. Dr. Mackintosh, in his work on the "Practice of Physic" (vol. i., page 141), writes that Dr. Halliday, of the India Company's Service, was, by order of the Marquis of Hastings, placed in arrest, and for several years deprived of his rank and pay, because he protested against the mercurial system of treating that disease. The fallacy of pushing that remedy, and bleeding to anything like the extent considered necessary towards the end of last century and early part of the present, has long since been acknowledged; yet the episode just related indicates the cost at which improvements in practice may be attended in the persons of their authors.

The following abstract of a case of the disease under notice will best indicate the means usually employed in treatment at the time of its occurrence, namely :—

Cumming, 10th foot, aged twenty-one, only three months in India, admitted into hospital 22nd September, 1867, suffering from ardent pyrexia and intense heat of the epigastrium ; he had been ill three days. There were indications of great congestion of the lower lobe of the left lung ; the tongue was brown and dry ; he laboured under a sense of general oppression ; the pulse was small and labouring. He was freely *soused* with water ; calomel and croton oil were administered, and leeches applied to the affected side. On the 26th he expressed himself as considerably relieved ; oppression was manifestly less ; the skin had become cooler, although the temperature at the epigastrium continued higher than at any other part of the surface. The state of the bowels continued relaxed. Ordinary diaphoretic mixture was ordered. On the 27th the appearance and sense of oppression had still further diminished ; pulse was small and contracted ; the sensation conveyed from the surface was more natural than it had been ; the tongue continued somewhat dry. Counter-irritation was now applied to the side, and the other treatment continued. On 30th September was expectorating tenacious mucus of a puriform character; all pyrexia gone. Had now quinine in small doses three times a day. On 4th October the expectoration had decreased ; no pain in the chest. The quinine, in one-grain doses, was continued. On the 10th he was reported as convalescent; expectoration had ceased; medicine omitted. On the 16th, the sounds in his chest were natural ; he felt well in all respects, and was accordingly discharged to duty.

Other illustrative cases might readily be given, but suffice it now to observe that not only is it usual to find the different manifestations of the disease differ at certain stations, but that the characters of the attacks, as witnessed at any locality in one year are often different from what they are at another. Thus, at one time the head will be chiefly implicated ; at another, the chest, and at a third, the viscera of the abdomen : the disease, consequently, requiring so many different methods of management.

In connection with the general subject of periodic fevers I would observe that, in so far as my individual experience of quinine has gone, I have not been led to form the superlatively high opinion of that remedy as an antidote or specific which many other medical officers, and doubtless, of more extended practice than myself, have expressed. I have already given statistics of intermittent fever, which seem to me to indicate that the power of quinine in checking that form has been overrated, and in my hands, I have never had reason to be satisfied with the advantages of ensuring a state of *cinchonism* over the milder, and, I think, more rational treatment by diaphoretics, evacuants, and the free use of cold water externally. I believe that to give a person suffering from the urgent symptoms of ardent, remittent, or of jungle fever, a half-drachm or two-scruple doses of quinine, and to repeat it after brief intervals, is merely to mask the symptoms which form part of either disease by those induced by the medicine itself; superadding, it is to be feared, the effects of the preparation to those of the influences upon which the disease originally depended, as we frequently see in persons whose inherent powers have enabled them to recover from both; as, for example, in deafness and loss of memory, to which they were for long periods afterwards subject. I have, in my own person, suffered severely from jungle fever and from intermittent fever; but in neither disease have I experienced much, if any, benefit from the use of quinine, while the effects of even small doses of the medicine, more especially in the latter, were of so unpleasant a nature that to me a paroxysm of the disease was really the less of two evils.

As a prophylactic of malarial fever, however, I join my belief with those who are advocates of its use. Unfortunately for the reputation of medicine as a science, it is a matter of difficulty to establish the direct connection between a particular remedy and effects ascribed to it; but from observation, under a considerable variety of circumstances, I have been led to consider that a judicious use of medicine wards off, if it does not altogether prevent, the recurrence of fevers of these descriptions.

Continued Fevers.

The forms of disease classed under the head of continued fevers include attacks of all degrees of severity, from the ephemeral paroxysm of pyrexia to that low, tedious, and exhausting malady which, having reduced the vital powers to the lowest ebb compatible with life, finally destroys them in a period varying from twenty to thirty days, or leaves the patient so debilitated and predisposed to recurrences of the same or other affections, that convalescence is not only tedious, but liable to numerous interruptions. In former times, and as probably is still the case, fever of the continued type prevailed to the greatest extent during the dry season. Young soldiers were especially liable to its attacks, so much so, that very few altogether escaped being subjected to it within the two first years of their residence in India. Its attacks are most common from March till October, both inclusive, and in one form or other occasions the greatest number of admissions into hospital of any disease met with in regimental practice; although not only is the mortality occasioned by it inconsiderable as compared with other endemic diseases, but remarkably so as compared with that of continued fevers in the United Kingdom. Thus, according to the documents to which I have had access, there were in the 10th Foot 4,044 admissions by this fever among soldiers, of whom 123 deaths, or a ratio of mortality to cases equal to 2·79 per cent.; among officers there were 218 admissions and 2 deaths, or 0·91 per cent.; among soldiers' wives 332 admissions and 10 deaths, or 3·01 per cent.; and among children, 156 admissions and 19 deaths, or 12·18 per cent. Here we see that in this, as in other diseases already noticed, the rate of mortality varies according to class. In the present instance it is shown to have been greatest among children, next among women, then among men, and least among officers; while, according to statistics, officers suffered in greatest proportion from its attacks, next men, then women, and least of all children.

Several years ago I had occasion to allude to the increase in this disease, as well as of others, among regiments in India, caused by what really was intended to be an act of liberality and consideration by the Government of that country. I then expressed myself as follows:*—

"It is painful to consider that the rewards sometimes given by a liberal Government, to troops who have been the means of bringing a campaign to a successful termination, may themselves prove a fertile cause of fever, as well as of some other diseases, claiming nearly as many, if not a quite equal number, as those who may have fallen honourably on the field of battle. For instance, the 10th

* *Medical Times and Gazette*, 1856.

Regiment, in the action at Sobraon, on the 10th February, 1846, lost in killed 29 men, in addition to 136 wounded, of whom six subsequently died in the Regimental Hospital. During 1845-46, the deaths from fevers of all kinds were 21. In the succeeding year—namely, 1846-47—the fatal cases of fevers amounted to 53, and of this number 40 occurred during the months of July, August, and September.

"In reference to this great mortality, we find, in the Hospital records, that suspicions were entertained that the drunkenness and exposure must have had a share in the sad work of destruction, as it was about this period that the Government donation batta (for Sobraon, &c.) was distributed. If, then, in this instance the supposition be allowed that of the 53 deaths that took place from fever in the 10th Regiment one half were solely attributable to the endemic influences which seem, in other seasons, to have given rise to the malady, it may, with equal propriety, be believed that the other half were occasioned by the drunkenness in which the men were enabled to indulge by the distribution of batta.

"The fact becomes, therefore, worthy of attention, that while the number of killed among one regiment at one of the most sanguinary of our Indian battles was only 29, no fewer than 26 lost their lives by only one form of disease, which more or less directly originated in consequence of the pecuniary rewards given for their services on that occasion."

I may observe, with reference to this matter, that not only in India, but at home, have I observed very serious evils to follow upon the issue of batta and other pecuniary donations to soldiers. Drunkenness and excesses of various kinds invariably follow upon such occasions; sickness and violence, whether accidental or intentional, destroy several lives; the health in other instances becomes permanently injured; crime is rampant, and men, some with families, who have for years led exemplary lives, and obtained promotion as the fitting reward, are, in an evil hour, led into temptation, the result of which is their own ruin and the after poverty and misery of all dependent upon them. From considerations such as these, I would therefore urge the desirability—nay, actual necessity—of abandoning the system of issuing to soldiers, who, with few exceptions, are improvident, sums of money which ouly afford them the means of injuring themselves morally and physically. It is right that certain rewards should be conferred upon men who have undergone the hardships and dangers of a campaign, but it is no less desirable that these rewards should not be made the means, by destroying discipline for the time, of impairing the efficiency of the service. Could both ends not be attained, then, by the institution of regulations under which batta, prize money, volunteering money, and all other casual allowances should be paid into a fund bearing interest, and only be at the personal disposal of the individual on his discharge, or under such restrictions as might be determined upon?

The usual manner in which an attack of continued fever occurs is something like this :—A soldier, probably young, of short residence in India, robust, and otherwise in good health, is brought to hospital suffering from ardent pyrexia, increased temperature of the surface, flushed face, throbbing headache, and so on. For two or three or more days he has felt "a little out of sorts ;" has been unable to take his meals ; has had an inclination to vomit, with "flying" pains here and there, but especially in his limbs and loins ; and these symptoms may have manifested themselves without sufficient evident cause, or, what is far more frequent, have succeeded to the simple exposure to the sun or exposure after drinking rum or native spirit—being subjected to wet, and then having to remain for a time without a change of clothes—or exposure to a chill at night ; and this last circumstance frequently happens as the hot season is setting in, or is about to give way to the cold. In either case the days and evenings are so warm that the soldier in India is induced to take his bed from his barrack room, and sleep either altogether outside or in the verandah. At first he is unable to bear much clothes upon him, and thus falls asleep. Towards morning, however, the cold increases, and by and bye awakes him ; he finds himself chilled, and at last, after repeated exposure in this way, is attacked with fever with or without catarrhal symptoms.

It may be proper here to observe that, while sleeping in the open air (in India) renders a person liable, during certain seasons of the year, to attacks of catarrh, continued fever, or ague, yet the prevalence of the habit among those who have been long in the country induces me to believe that during other seasons, especially the hot winds, when hardly any moisture exists in the atmosphere, not only is it unattended with danger, but is actually beneficial.

For three months in the year the heat of the air is such that persons who have not themselves experienced it cannot conceive its intensity. Within doors, the ordinary contrivances employed for cooling it will reduce the temperature of a room to 87° F., while the thermometer outside exposed to the sun will range above 140° F. ; so that the sensations of a person on first going into an apartment so cooled are probably about what a Russian experiences when he throws himself from his warm bath into snow.

Soldiers, however, have not the art, neither have they always the means, of thus lowering the temperature of their barracks, the walls of which speedily become heated to such a degree that the sensations are oppressed on going near them, and anything seems preferable to sleeping in such an oven. Nor do I think it would be advisable in any way that they should be forced against their will to remain inside.

In some parts of the world, where the land wind surcharged with the germs of disease sweeps over unhealthy swamps, and comes loaded with pernicious matters, blowing from evening till sunrise, it would be madness in any person to sleep out of doors, and most improper in officers to permit such a habit among troops. Neither can it be practised in many parts of Lower Bengal without risk ; but away from lakes or swamps, with a clear dry atmosphere, as in the upper provinces of India, these objections do not hold good.

The more I have seen of diseases affecting the general system, such as fevers, the more am I convinced that their characters vary according to locality. Nor ought this fact to be forgotten in the management of cases that come under our observation. So long as the febrile action continues ardent and uncomplicated with any particular amount of local deterioration, we have in common continued fever little to fear; the attack will in all probability wear off in a short time, leaving no other effect than a little temporary debility. But let us beware of those cases where particular affections of the viscera of either of the large cavities become implicated, or where, with or without treatment, the first symptoms speedily give place to those of debility or collapse; and let our treatment be so directed that, while our measures are employed with a view to subdue the febrile symptoms, we may, nevertheless, keep the case in hand, so to speak, as to be ready to combat whatever tendency it may assume, to change or modify its original character.

In the treatment of this very prevalent disease we must be cautious, in administering even the lowering medicines that are indicated, lest their effect should be to induce a state of weakness or complete collapse, from which much difficulty may be experienced in recovering the patient.

Cold affusion is a remedy equally valuable during the continuance of ardent pyrexia in one fever as in another; and the gratefulness of the measure to the sensations of the patient, and its powerful effect in inducing a remission, followed by refreshing sleep, ought always to be borne in view.

After the first intensity of the pyrexia has given way, and the pulse become reduced in frequency and force, the skin cool, and the patient has perhaps fallen asleep, it is essential in all cases, even the most trivial, that caution be exercised in the degree to which lowering medicines are pushed; and in order to guard against dangerous depression, it will be necessary carefully to watch the case, in order that the first tendency to such exhaustion may be combated by appropriate remedies.

When such a tendency does manifest itself, a combination of quinine, æther, and camphor will generally be found to be the most useful remedy in restoring the normal state of vital action, and in diminishing what disposition may still remain to febrile attack. It is impossible to lay down definite rules as to the proper interval between the doses, or the length of time a particular remedy ought to be continued; but a repetition of the above every hour until a definite effect is produced, increasing the intervals while necessary, may, perhaps, be deemed the most appropriate instructions in such a case.

It frequently happens in cases of fever, such as occur in India, that a degree of debility remains, after the disappearance of the primary disease, altogether out of proportion in degree to what might be expected from the severity in the first instance. Tonics, nourishing diet, wine, or spirits must, therefore, be given according to the necessities of individual cases; and it will be well if we learn early in our military practice not to treat all our patients, whose diseases are referable to a certain head in our returns, upon one principle of routine; for in no class of affections so much as in fevers does it become necessary that we should not be blindly led by school and theoretic impressions, but should learn to think for ourselves, and make allowances for individual peculiarities, the nature of the prevailing disease in particular years and in particular localities.

During convalescence, mild tonics, a weak mixture of quinine, or decoction of cinchona, with a moderate allowance of wine or beer, and light nutritious diet, form the most appropriate measures. We ought to be cautious in permitting the patient to get out of bed too early, in order to avoid the danger of a relapse; but when this may be permitted, gentle airing, as in a dooly, will be beneficial.

I am not aware of any point in the treatment of fever in India on which it is necessary to caution the young medical officer so much as on the administration of stimulants. Bringing their home opinions with them, it is by no means uncommon to find them in all cases of fever, even in the ardent remittent, giving large quantities of wine during the continuance of high states of pyrexia ; and in such, as might be expected, the danger that always exists of the disease becoming transformed into heat apoplexy is increased, at the same time that the proper opportunity is lost for employing the more appropriate remedies.

Indeed, the employment of diffusible stimuli in early stages of the affection, while inducing excitement of the powers for a time, would seem either to increase whatever tendency there may be to cerebral affection, or at least protract the period of pyrexia.

It is not intended by these remarks to deny the utility of wine in the cases under consideration. All that is desired is to inculcate the necessity of caution in its use. In the great majority of instances, however, we find that the employment of beef-tea, jugged soups, with the usual tonics, will be sufficient until the commencement of convalescence, after which much discrimination is necessary in directing the further progress of the patient towards complete recovery.

Fevers of the typhus or typhoid type are, and have always been, very rare among British soldiers in India. The presence of both these diseases, however, has been observed and reported by army surgeons many years ago, although, on account of cleanliness and free ventilation observed in barracks and cantonments, no more than seven cases of the former affection appear to have been noted in the statistics of the 10th Regiment during thirteen years in that country, and they occurred while the corps was quartered in close unsuitable places in Lahore, immediately subsequent to the first Punjaub war. According to statistics of the corps, one case occurred under these circumstances in 1847-8, one in 1848-9, and five in 1850-1 ; and, although information is somewhat scanty in regard to the conditions under which the men were at the time placed, the following remarks by the surgeon at that time may even still have considerable value :—

He states that, at the commencement of the hot season (of 1847), when the regiment occupied the places just mentioned, numbers of men were driven into hospital by an endemic fever of the continued and remittent type ; its invasion marked by great prostration of strength, rigors, and flushings, succeeded by augmented heat of the surface, increased external action, and aching pains all over the body.

When taken in time it yielded rapidly to moderate depletion, antimonials, and quinine. The fatal cases were not numerous from this cause, and generally resulted in typhoid symptoms.

This last remark would naturally lead to the belief that the cases returned as "typhus" do not in reality represent the degree to which such prevailed ; and it must be confessed that more extended and minute statistics than are in my possession must be supplied before the actual prevalence of typhus fever among our troops in India can be ascertained.

Heat Apoplexy.

Under the term *heat apoplexy* I would include the affections severally described as erythismus tropicus, coup-de-soleil, apoplexy of the hot winds, sun-stroke, &c., &c. ; for although, according to some authors, an essential difference exists between them, my own experience induces me to believe that they are in reality identical—all mere manifestations of derangements in vital functions arising from similar causes, but modified by conditions in which their subject is at the time placed. In all, the symptoms are the same, the treatment alike, and the *post-mortem* appearances undistinguishable, while in none are they sufficient to account either for the indications present during life, or for the fatal result in persons who die.

In former years the disease was attended by frightful

mortality. In the 10th Regiment, for example, 28 cases were recorded as having occurred prior to 1857, one patient only surviving, and he so shattered in health as to have been unfitted for further service. Some other corps suffered far more severely than this from the disease, the recoveries being no more numerous relatively. I cannot help thinking that the greater prevalence of spirit drinking in former years, as compared with more recent times, conduced in a great measure to this prevalence and mortality; while among other circumstances which led to the same result may be enumerated the overcrowding of men in barracks then practised, the want of artificial means of cooling their rooms, and the system of enforced confinement of the soldiers to their barracks without any means of occupation or amusement during nearly twenty out of every twenty-four hours throughout several months of the year. Thanks to the frequent and energetic representations of army medical officers, all such conditions are now much improved, if not altogether done away with; and the result is a material decrease in the prevalence of this disease, as well as of some others to which, in the course of these notes, allusion has already been made. In fact, we learn by the Departmental Blue Book for 1866 that, during the year, only 162 cases of the affection were recorded in the army serving in India, of which number 72 were fatal.

I believe that the term "sun-stroke" first applied to the malady was unfortunate, and that it has been productive of error in the manner of managing the sanitation of soldiers. Needless fear of simple out-door exposure was fostered by reason of the appellation. The facts must have been patent formerly, as they still are, that the victims of attacks were most numerous among soldiers who were compulsorily confined, whether in barracks, cells, or hospital; and that indigo planters, as well as other Europeans whose vocations necessitated much out-door exposure, were seldom subjects of sun-stroke, yet I question if the opinion be even now quite exploded, that the only means by which soldiers can be protected from this disease is their seclusion in darkened and imperfectly ventilated rooms, such as barracks afford, notwithstanding all the more recent improvements in their construction.

Doubtless, the truth of these views was sorely tried during the mutiny. It was amply shown, during the operations connected with that outbreak, that soldiers could perform long marches and fight battles in the hottest weather without necessarily being attacked by this disease, although, on the other hand, they were under certain conditions extremely prone to its attacks. Thus it was found that, so long as the men were absolutely without ardent spirits or other intoxicating drinks, and were provided on the line of march with an abundant supply of water, they could undergo a very considerable degree of exertion under the fierce sun of an Indian summer ; and here I may observe that, on some of the longest marches in the hot season, it was found necessary to have elephants, camels, and bullocks carrying skins filled with water, brought along with the regiment ; and men as well as officers, all alike lightly clothed, were in the habit from time to time of allowing a free stream from those skins to fall upon them, soaking them from head downwards. By such means the functions of the skin were maintained, and the temperature of the surface kept at a moderate elevation. Among other effects also produced was probably the supply by this means of oxygen to the blood circulating in the superficial capillaries. On the other hand, however, it was found in the case of some corps that men when debilitated, whether by insufficient food, by long-continued physical fatigue, or morally depressed through only partial success against the rebel enemy, were by no means thus exempt from its attacks ; while the well-known liability to the disease manifested by men sick in hospital and undergoing punishment in cells may be accounted for on the same principle.

With regard to the period of the day at which persons are most liable to become attacked by the disease, I believe experience indicates this to be chiefly the later part of the afternoon and early part of the night. In either case the seizure is most to be dreaded during the time its subject is asleep, and especially when upon exhaustion is superadded heavy meals or potations of spirits. But, then, it by no means happens that cases of the disease are in proportion to the heat of the weather. Dry heat, more especially if the atmosphere be in rapid movement, is not so productive of attacks as a more moderate temperature, with a high ratio of aqueous vapour in suspension, and an absence of wind. Under such circumstances, and when the sky becomes obscured by dark negatively electric clouds, cases are tolerably certain to occur if the temperature in the shade be 97° F. and upwards; and, in fact, old residents come to know by their own sensations the conditions under which those who are predisposed to the malady are most liable to its attack. In the far inland districts of India, for example, all recognize such conditions in those calm sultry days which occasionally occur during the period of the hot winds, when the sun is obscured by a film of cloud, or by the impalpable dust suspended in the atmosphere. Nor is it man alone who, under such conditions, becomes subject to the disease; domestic animals, quadrupeds, and birds suffer equally with him, and the longer a dust or thunder storm is then delayed, the greater will be the mortality by the affection.

Medical officers are aware that many cases occur, especially during the hot and rainy season, in which it becomes difficult to decide whether the symptoms of the patient are referable to remittent fever or to heat apoplexy; while in others, symptoms which appear to characterize only the former run into the more dangerous conditions of the latter. From this circumstance alone, however, I question if we may rightly conclude that the origin of the "apoplexy" is traceable to malaria; in fact, there appears to be every reason for the belief that such is not the case, but that the affection, as well as the ardent fever, primarily arise from conditions of the atmosphere altogether unconnected with the presence of paludal emanations, inasmuch as the prevailing high temperature under which it occurs is destructive of such emanations—a circumstance which, as already observed, indicates a want of identity between the actual nature of the ardent remittent and the marsh remittent fever prevailing in different parts of the country.

I have remarked that, in the case of men, the affection is of common occurrence among those who, from whatever cause, remain much in confinement. In the case of women, however, this is different, and it is of some importance to note the circumstance. There were in the 10th Regiment an average of ninety soldiers' wives annually, and during twelve years no case of the affection is mentioned as having occurred among them. An explanation of this exemption is doubtless to be found in the nature of a woman's occupation in-doors, as compared with man's. The wife, in performing the duties connected with her establishment, however small it may be, has sufficient bodily occupation to employ without fatiguing her, at the same time that her attention is also engaged; whereas, the soldier who voluntarily spends his time within doors is usually idle, perhaps a glutton or a drunkard; he passes the hours in idleness or in sleep; and the latter habit indulged in after heavy meals or a debauch of drink is one of the most powerful among the predisposing causes of the disease. I may here remark that, so far as I am aware, the wives of officers under the ordinary conditions of their class enjoy complete exemption from the affection.

It is a fact which deserves to be noted that, throughout the operations in the field in which the 10th Foot was engaged in connection with the Indian mutiny, no case of heat apoplexy among the men is recorded in the hospital records from the 1st of April, 1857, to the 31st of March, 1858. Other regiments were, however, less fortunate, and in one corps a heavy loss by the disease occurred among a detachment of men who, after a debauch during the night, marched during a day in the hot season, heavily accoutred and thickly clothed. But in the three succeeding months of 1858 our soldiers were not so exempt from the disease. By that time they had become physically lowered to a considerable extent, and thus their predisposition to attack increased. In a strength of 535 men, eleven cases occurred during April, May, and June, 1858, of which two only proved fatal. This proportion of mortality, if compared with that in previous years, might at first sight give rise to the impression that the attacks which happened were relatively slight. Such, however, was by no means the case; on the other hand, none were referred to heat apoplexy, except those in which actual insensibility was present.

The manner in which the attack by the disease occurs is various. In a considerable number of cases the person during sleep seems to pass gradually into the affection, the first indication of which is discovered in his stertorous breathing, and the intense and peculiar heat which prevails over the surface generally; in others, the affection, as already observed, supervenes upon a paroxysm of fever, the line of demarcation between the one and the other being often drawn with difficulty; in a third class of cases, the approach of the attack is indicated by the vacancy of expression, flushed face, and unusual behaviour of the patient; and in yet another class of cases, the person threatened with the attack is himself the first to mention the peculiar sensations which he experiences; these being, for the most part, weakness in and want of power over the lower extremities, involuntary micturition, giddiness or fulness in the head, and confused ideas. During the time of the mutiny, several instances of the latter occurred among officers, as well as among men, but by the early and free use of the douche the further advance of the disease was checked. The cases were not recorded as those of heat apoplexy, because the conditions had not become complete; but I do not now remember that of any person thus affected who had not to be sent to England at the first favourable opportunity. It is, no doubt, of such that we are accustomed to hear a good deal as having suffered from sun-stroke, and although a large number make speedy and perfect recoveries in the more favourable climate of

Britain, it is beyond question that many others remain in the state of invalids for years.

In what manner we are to account for the intense and peculiar heat of epigastrium and surface generally in this disease becomes a problem the solution of which is difficult. It deserves the fullest attention on the part of medical officers. In all probability, a direct connection will be found to exist between it and the deranged condition of the functions of circulation and respiration, which constitute an important part of the malady; thus, while during life the skin is so dry as to be utterly incapable of performing its functions as an emunctory, *post-mortem* examination reveals extensive pulmonary and cardiac congestion, the mass of blood at the same time indicating a state of imperfect decarbonisation. Doubtless, the insufficient *combustion* of carbon furnishes by itself an insufficient explanation of increased temperature, but all that I desire to indicate is, that a field for inquiry is here open.

Until a period comparatively recent, so uniformly fatal was this disease that it was considered as being absolutely beyond the power of treatment. Of late, however, as already observed, the results are more favourable, and we are now able to employ remedies with as much hope of success as in any other of the more important maladies which affect our soldiers in India. Having, some years ago, entered somewhat fully into the history of heat apoplexy,* it will suffice for my present purpose if I allude to the fact that, when the custom was to bleed freely from a vein, the patient being retained in the sitting posture, death occurred in all cases of the affection, the event often taking place while the patient was in the act of undergoing the depletion. How far this may have been connected with the treatment itself, it were needless now to discuss; but we cannot forget that, at the time referred to, not only were soldiers much more crowded together in their barrack-rooms than they now are, but so preva-

* See *Edinburgh Medical Journal*, May, 1860.

lent among them was the vice of spirit drinking, that we may fairly presume these powerful causes of the affection occasioned not only more severe attacks, but of a more virulent nature than are, as a rule, now met with. I believe that my present purpose will be served by the following cases, which illustrate the manner of treating the affection which recent experience indicates to be most generally successful, and which may, in brief, be said to include—1. Free affusion over the whole body, but more especially the head and epigastrium; 2. Free abstraction of blood from the temporal arteries; 3. Internal counter-irritation, as by the administration of croton oil; and, 4. External counter-irritation, as by sudden vesication of the nape, sinapisms to the calves of the legs, &c.

Let us suppose, for example, that a patient was first seen when labouring under confirmed heat apoplexy, all the symptoms of which were complete; the manner of procedure was somewhat thus:—He was immediately brought on a bedstead outside the ward, and freely *soused* with water poured upon him from a height, and, if possible, by two persons at the same time; for a few minutes the shock was produced, as far as practicable, by directing the current upon his head and epigastrium, and if, as sometimes occurred, the unconscious man was capable of swallowing, cold water was put to his lips or into his mouth. He was next turned upon his face, and similar affusion applied along the spine, friction being by attendants made to his legs. If, in the meantime, he could be induced to swallow several drops of croton oil, it was considered so much the better; but if not, some four or five upon powdered sugar were placed in the mouth while he lay upon his back, in the hope of some of it finding its way, as it often did, into the stomach, producing vomiting or free catharsis. One or both the temporal arteries were meantime opened and allowed to bleed, while the affusion and frictions were continued, it being found that no risk whatever existed of depletion being thus carried too far, inasmuch as the hæmorrhage ceased spontaneously, if not checked artificially. When, however, these remedies failed to produce effect, sinapisms were applied to the legs, and vesication on the nape produced by the application for an instant of a heated spatula.

These are energetic remedies, and they must be energetically employed. We no more can look for success in recovering a soldier rendered unconscious by an attack of heat apoplexy by the employment of such means applied for a short time and in an undecided manner, than we can expect to restore animation in a person asphyxiated by immersion in water by mild remedies. If, therefore, a medical officer be too apathetic or indifferent to fairly grapple with this disease, and leave his patient to the care of imperfectly instructed attendants, or to the languid attentions of native Asiatics, it is right that such a man should know that the soldier thus affected with heat apoplexy, and thus left, will to a certainty die. I have seen instances of the apathy and indifference to which I allude, not only in the treatment of this disease, but in that of others of fearful virulence. I have seen, as a matter of course, the results to be expected from such indiffereuce, and it is because I have wituessed them that I now express myself as I do.

The case given below was the first I had the satisfaction of treating successfully :—

Private Jeremiah McCarthy, aged thirty years, admitted at Wuzeerabad, in the Punjaub, 7th October, 1852, suffering from giddiness in the head and general debility. Had been subject a few days previously to diarrhœa. On the forenoon of the following day, he was found lying in the rear in a state of insensibility, and with all the symptoms of apoplexy of the hot winds ; there was much suffusion of the eyes and the countenance ; the temporal arteries were distended ; the epigastrium was very pungently hot, and he kept constantly striking that region with his hand during his insensibility ; he was voiding fæces involuntarily in bed. He remained in this state for a period of upwards of two hours before treatment was employed ; the remedial measures had reeourse to were opening the right temporal artery ; eold affusion to the head and epigastrie region ; slight cautery to the nape. It having been observed, during the state of unconsciousness, that he indicated a desire to drink, eold water was given, and he imbibed it with avidity. After he had bled to probably twelve ounees, eonseiousness began to return. He then had a dose of eroton oil and calomel, and in the eourse of a few minutes afterwards he was able to answer questions rationally ; complaining, however, of a sensation of weight and giddiness in the head. The following is an extraet of his ease from the medical register :—

October 10th.—Considerably better this morning ; pulse moderate ; skin eool ; respiration natural ; slept well during the night. ℞ Hyd. ehlor., gr. ij. ; pulv. ant. eo., gr. ij., ter in die.

11th.—Pulse moderate ; tongue furred ; doing well, but is weak. ℞ Aeid. sulph. dil., ♏x. ; inf. chirettæ, ℥j., ter in die.

12th.—Pulse moderate ; tongue furred ; eomplains eonsiderably of pain and swelling of the epigastrium. Cont. med., et app. emp. vesieat. epigastrium.

13th.—The pain of epigastrium eonsiderably less ; tongue less furred ; pulse still weak. Cont. med., ter in die.

14th.—Tongue eleaner and moister ; pulse stronger ; does not complain of any epigastrie pain. Cont. med., ter in die.

15th.—The same remark applies.

16th.—Is now perfeetly free from epigastrie pain ; gums swollen ; breath very fetid (mereurial).

The recovery of this man was so far eomplete that he was subsequently sent to England as an invalid, and discharged the service ; but so unexpeeted at the time of his illness was any other result than death in the ease of a person attacked as he was, that, when I had seen him, the rites usually performed over the dying by priests of the denomination to which he belonged had been administered; and I was so unfortunate as to incur much ill-feeling because I had been the means of restoring a man who should, it seems, according to all "spiritual" rules, have "gone, we know not where."

The following cases occurred during the mutiny—namely:—

Johnston, 10th Foot, forty years of age, sixteen in India; a hard drinker, although he had enjoyed good health. On the 6th of May, 1858, he was, in all respects, in apparent good health. On the 7th, the field force employed near Arrah marched at daylight, and continued to do so till about ten a.m., he accompanying it. About eight o'clock he was observed to stagger in the ranks, and in other respects his manner was so strange that his captain, mistaking the cause, ordered him into arrest. The morning was extremely hot and oppressive, and, as our route was westward, the direct rays of the sun fell upon the backs of all. He having been ordered to the rear, he doubtless intended to wait till that part of the regiment should come to him. He did so, and was found by the guard lying by the roadside, in a partially unconscious condition; he was nearly pulseless; the breathing was hurried and gasping; the temperature of the surface was natural; there was no distension of the temporal arteries; the face was somewhat pallid; pupils contracted. Affusion was applied to the head, and had the effect, for a minute or so, of rousing him to consciousness. He fell back to his former condition, however; in about half an hour from this time his face and surface had become livid; he moaned heavily, but without stertor; and almost instantaneously died.

His case may be considered as an example of the manner in which death by this disease occurs, after direct exposure to solar influence, in the person of a man who had been for years an habitual drinker of ardent spirits.

Maher, 10th Foot, twenty years of age, seven months in India; not of very full habits; admitted into hospital on 24th May, 1858, while on service against the Sepoys in Jugdespore jungles. In the forenoon of that day marched with a portion of the regiment against the enemy, but at three p.m. was brought back to camp apoplectic, he having suddenly fallen down in the ranks an hour previous, with the well-known symptoms of heat apoplexy. On being brought to hospital, unconsciousness was complete ; the surface of the body was less hot than is usually the case during attacks of the disease ; the hands were firmly clenched, the thumb of the left being drawn across the palm, that of the right was semi-flexed ; the conjunctivæ were much suffused ; the eyes slightly turned upwards ; pupils contracted and insensible ; he moaned heavily ; breathing was heavy, and at times stertorous ; much froth issued from the mouth ; the pulse was variable, at one time scarcely perceptible, at another wavy, but not rapid ; the face and general surface were congested and bloated.

Affusion was immediately employed to the head and epigastrium. The right temporal artery was opened, and allowed to bleed, the patient being in the recumbent position while affusion was continued. Five grains of calomel and five drops of croton oil were placed upon the tongue, and on applying a jug of water to the lips he swallowed a few mouthfuls. Shortly afterwards he vomited freely a quantity of green bile and mucus ; the pulse assumed a more regular rhythm ; the bleeding from the artery ceased spontaneously, and he appeared slightly conscious. The affusion was now repeated, as also the dose of calomel and croton oil, and an enema of turpentine administered. About five p.m. vesication on the nape was instantaneously produced by the application of a hot spatula ; he was kept cool, and about seven o'clock fell asleep. At eight p.m. he was found conscious ; skin not very hot ; bowels had been profusely moved ; pulse natural ; and the expression of the face so much improved that he did not look like the same person who had, a few hours before, been brought to hospital. His recovery was rapid and complete.

I have given one fatal case, my object being to indicate the usual course of this very alarming disease. Many such must occur under any method of treatment, and especially when, as in that given, the subject of the attack had been for years of intemperate habits. I believe, however, that by following the plan of treatment I have indicated, a satisfactory degree of success will be obtained. Such was the case in my hands, and in those of other medical officers who adopted it ; but, as I said before, so I repeat, neither it nor any other plan will be successful if guided by apathy, indifference, or indecision.

Paralytic Affections.

According to regimental statistics it would seem that paralytic affections are less common among soldiers in India than in that portion of our army stationed in the United Kingdom, a circumstance in some measure to be accounted for by the fact that diseases implicating the cerebro-spinal system in that country usually occur with such severity as to destroy life before the lesions upon which paralysis directly depends have had time to occur. Thus, no more than 28 cases among soldiers, and 2 in officers, are borne on the records of the 10th Foot throughout thirteen years' service on the Bengal side, none appearing to have occurred either among the wives or children of soldiers ; although the same documents show the prevalence and mortality of the entire class of diseases affecting the nervous system to have been 288 cases, of which 53 were fatal among men ; 16, and 3 fatal, among officers ; 19, and 2 deaths, among women ; 31, and 18 deaths, among children. Among the two latter classes of persons no case of paralysis in any form seems to have happened. Information is unfortunately wanting as to the precise nature of the affection in the case of the officers whose deaths occurred from this cause ; but the soldier who died paralytic was a man who had, for a considerable time, suffered from secondary syphilis, on which lesion of the spinal cord doubtless depended. He gradually lost the power of motion in the lower extremities, and finally sank under diarrhœa and bed-sores.

It is not to be supposed, however, that because the rate of mortality by these affections was so small as is here represented, persons once their subjects returned after a time to their duty. Such was by no means the case. On the contrary, it does not appear that any instances of recovery really took place, although I do not see why, in some instances, at any rate, of local paralysis, as of the wrist or eyelid, the proper functions of the parts may not be restored. In cases of paraplegia or hemiplegia, especially if occurring as independent affections, although medical treatment may produce some degree of benefit, it is hopeless to look for recovery in India. The subjects should, in all cases, be despatched to England by the first favourable opportunity.

The particular influences upon which paralysis in some cases depends, or, in other words, its *exciting causes*, are in many cases obscure; so much so, that cases of the affection implicating entire limbs, or isolated portions of them, are often referred, by natives and Europeans long resident in the country, to the mere passage of currents of hot air across them. The effect of direct solar heat upon the head or loins is more apparent, and we observe attacks of the affection following upon partial seizures of heat apoplexy. Nor is it alone in man that this is believed to occur. Horses are said to be particularly prone to partial paralysis of the hinder extremities from the effect of solar heat upon the spinal marrow, to prevent which it is customary to protect their loins by heavy folds of cloth while picketed, as they usually are. Perhaps a similar belief, whether formed with or without reason, has led to the employment by natives of the waist cloth, or *cummerbund*—an article of dress found by several of us to have afforded great comfort during the exposure to which we were subjected in the Indian mutiny.

It has been asserted that, by a careful observation of the conditions attending paralysis of the lower extremities, the nature and seat of the lesion to which they owe their origin may be ascertained. For example, if in the application of an irritant to the foot, involuntary contraction of the limb take place, the lesion may be considered to exist in the upper part of the cord; if they are not exerted, then it either is confined to, or has descended to, the lower portion of the cord. Then, again, as to the conditions upon which paralysis depends, the following rules have been laid down*—namely :—

1. If incomplete and with spasms, it probably arises from meningitis, cerebral or spinal.

2. If gradual and with contraction of the flexors, from cerebral or spinal softening of inflammatory nature.

3. If gradual and without contraction of the flexors from non-inflammatory cerebral or spinal softening.

4. If sudden and again suddenly disappearing, from temporary congestion.

5. If persistent and with epileptic symptoms, from hæmorrhage.

How far these arbitrary rules are trustworthy I have not personally tested; nevertheless, as they are deserving of notice I give them here for the benefit of medical officers in India.

Shaking Palsy, or paralysis agitans, is seldom met with among soldiers, probably for this reason, that this form is chiefly a disease of the more advanced in life. All the cases of this form which came under observation in India occurred in men of long service in that country, and were addicted either to spirit drinking or to opium eating. In none of them, however, was the attack of a nature to require their admission into hospital, although in all it disqualified them for further duty. And having alluded to the vice of opium-eating, I would observe that it is, in all probability, less prevalent among our soldiers in India than it was in former years. Even so lately as 1854 there

* See Wood's "Practice of Medicine," p. 862. Vol. II.

were in the 10th Foot several old soldiers who were habitual opium-eaters, and there was every reason to believe that the vice was no less prevalent in other regiments. The system of "relief" of regiments now in force renders the style of persons formerly known as the "old Indian soldier" an institution of the past, and at the same time probably effects considerable changes in the habits of the men; yet that there are still some who indulge in the use of opium, not only in India, but for some time after their return to the United Kingdom, I have ascertained, and been further informed of the ingenuity practised by them in the manner in which they smuggle the drug into England, by having their boots provided with false soles before leaving India, and filling the intervening space with the narcotic.

Local Palsy.—Of the various kinds of local paralysis, those most commonly met with in India among soldiers are paralysis of one side of the face, ptosis, and wrist-drop. This form may even be confined to a finger or a phalanx, and in all cases is generally attributed to the effects of "a stroke of the wind," or, in other words, its precise cause is obscure. In addition to the above forms of paralysis, it is by no means unfrequent in India to meet with instances in which a person recovering from severe malarious fever, finds that one or more of his limbs are attacked with this form of disease, sensation being in some cases unaffected, in others impaired, in others increased; while, in other instances, the sensation of different sides of the body is deranged in such a manner, that, for example, water being applied gives a sensation of heat to one and cold to another limb. The disease in these cases has been referred respectively to the presence of inflammatory action in the nervous centres, to what has been termed "impaired nervous power," and to the poisonous effects of malaria in the system. In all such cases recovery is slow. The patient must in all cases proceed to a temperate climate, where, under suitable regimen, recovery after some years may be complete, although the instances are by no means rare in which the subjects of the disease never fully recover the full power of the affected part.

Epilepsy.—This disease, like the class of affections last described, would appear to occur less frequently among soldiers in India than in those stationed in the United Kingdom. Probably one cause of this difference exists in the circumstance that the disease, being one chiefly of early manhood, recruits are rejected when suspected to be, or are actually suffering from it, so that they do not reach the country; yet that another cause for the comparative exemption probably exists seems to be indicated by the fact that, according to regimental statistics, no case of the affection is recorded among the children during thirteen years' service of the corps in different parts of India. The children of soldiers there are, as a rule, better fed, and possibly better taken care of in other ways than are those of the poorer classes in Britain ; and this circumstance may also diminish their liability to epilepsy. Yet there is another and probably a more constant cause of the difference than either of these, namely, the probability that children who have an existing tendency to cerebral disease, like "those whom the gods love, die young." Acute hydrocephalus, or convulsions, destroy them before they have reached the age when epilepsy usually supervenes.

The affection seems also to be of comparatively rare occurrence among soldiers' wives and among officers, and when happening among soldiers themselves seldom destroys life, although it unfits a man for continuing in the army, when occurring as an idiopathic affection. Cases do occur, although not frequently, in which an apparently pure attack of the disease follows upon a debauch, or is directly traceable to the irritation caused by intestinal worms, especially the long worm and the ascarides. These cases, however, are, for the most part, readily distinguished. Among other causes which induce the disease in India, local injuries are not unfrequent, while cases of the affection are by no means rare in persons who have undergone a severe attack of "jungle" or marsh remittent fever, or have been subjects of sunstroke.

Mental Affections.

During the first year the 10th Regiment was in India only one case of mental disorder occurred, and it of melancholia. In the second year there were four, namely, three of monomania, supposed to be due to intemperance, and one of melancholia, attributed to the patient having at one time received a blow on the head. In the third there were three cases, namely, one of monomania, the result of intemperance; one of melancholia, from injury to the head; and one in whom the affection was assumed, the malingerer being subsequently sent back to duty. Only one case occurred in the fourth and fifth year, the nature of which is not recorded; but the fact may be noted that, in the former of these, the regiment was engaged in an arduous campaign against the Sikhs, and went through several well-contested battles. In the sixth year one case occurred, namely, of amentia, the cause of which was not apparent; but the attack was temporary, the patient having recovered within the twelve months. The following year, however—that is, the seventh—five cases, all of amentia, occurred, the causes of attack being in all obscure. In the eighth, two cases, both of mania, occurred. The cause was in one obscure, and the patient had to be invalided; in the other, the attack was attributable to intemperance, and the patient recovered. Four cases, all of amentia, occurred in the ninth year. In one drink was the cause, and the patient had to be invalided; in the three remaining cases the cause of the affection was obscure. Two of the patients recovered, and one was sent to England as an invalid. In the tenth year two cases occurred, namely, one of amentia, arising from intemperance and repeated attacks of delirium tremens, the patient being subsequently sent home as incurable; the other, a case of mania, seems in reality to have occurred in a person labouring under ordinary phrenitis. In the eleventh year three cases came under notice. In one the symptoms were suspicious, so much so that the patient was only taken under observation; after a time, however, he manifested symptoms of mania and died of phrenitis. The second case was feigned, its subject ultimately returning to his duty. The third case was, to say the least, suspicious, and happened in a soldier who, there was every reason to believe, had determined to incapacitate himself from military service, although with the alternative of being transported for life. With this view he struck a non-commissioned officer, and, while being medically examined as to his fitness to undergo punishment, then struck me. I myself raised the question of his sanity, more with a view to shield him against the probable consequences of his offence, seeing that assaults upon officers were at the time becoming so frequent that sentence of death had at last to be carried into execution to put a stop to them. This soldier was acquitted of his crime on the plea of insanity, and sent to the Government Lunatic Asylum. After remaining there a year he was discharged to join his regiment, but while *en route* died of cholera. In the twelfth year three men, labouring under anomalous symptoms, were taken under observation; two of them ultimately returned to their duty, but the third having been retained many months under observation, under the belief that he was simulating insanity, became affected with low fever, under which he rapidly succumbed. In the thirteenth and last year to which my records extend, five cases of mental affection came under observation. In two of them the form of disease was unquestionably amentia, but in three the symptoms were of such a nature as to cause some suspicion regarding their real nature.

If now we analyse the abstract just given, we find that in the period mentioned there occurred in the 10th Foot fifteen cases of amentia, of which five terminated in reco-
disease was unquestionably amentia, but in three the symp-.

There was one case of mania, the patient dying of phrenitis. Five cases of monomania were recorded, the patients in all being invalided. There were two of melancholia, also invalided. There were eight in which the symptoms were more or less suspicious ; of these, one patient died of phrenitis, one of fever, two returned to duty, one was sent to a lunatic asylum on conviction of a military crime, and three remained under observation.

It would appear by the regimental returns that the cases of melancholic form of mental disorder were of most frequent occurrence during the earlier period of the Indian service of their subjects. If such be actually the case, it is quite in accordance with what might be expected ; but in all probability it needs further confirmation, as does also the equally popular impression that cases of suicide are in proportion more frequent among Scotch soldiers than in either the English or Irish. I do not now remember any instance in which a soldier of the 10th Regiment attempted suicide during the time to which my notes refer. It would seem that the causes which lead some to shorten their own lives had with them the effect of producing personal recklessness, ending in crimes of violence against others, and in outbreaks of dissipation ; and this leads me to remark that there are at times episodes in the history of men who enlist as soldiers sufficient in themselves to account for many acts of desperation of which they are guilty before the final act is perpetrated which terminates the period of their personal liberty, or induces the illness which removes them by death or invaliding from the army. I had occasion to see a striking illustration of the truth of this remark while stationed at Wuzzeerabad, in the Punjaub, in 1851. Shortly after I had been struck by a soldier, as already mentioned, the Surgeon of the 3rd Light Dragoons, then occupying the same station, was, while visiting the sick, severely assaulted by a soldier of the corps, then a patient in the hospital. Dr. Henderson, desirous, if possible, to save the man from the legal consequences of his offence, suggested that a Board of Medical Officers should meet to inquire into the state of the man's mind. I was President of the Board so assembled, and perhaps on that account was selected by the unfortunate soldier to listen to the sad tale he had to relate. His name was Brown, at least that was the name by which he was known in the 3rd Dragoons. According to his own account, he and a bricklayer's apprentice of the name of (assumed or real) of Eaton, one Sunday night in 1845, while walking along Wandsworth Common, met a drunken sailor. Both of them were at the time "hard up." They had been drinking, and the sight of the sailor, who seemed as if he had come off a long voyage, tempted them to think of robbery and murder. The double crime was speedily carried into execution, and Brown related to me in all their minuteness the means by which they were perpetrated, adding that the proceeds amounted to £40 in money, together with a gold watch and chain. He further informed me that the money and watch were retained, but the chain disposed of in a shop in one of the streets near Drury lane Theatre. In order to dispose of the body a spade was robbed from a house at some distance, a grave dug, and during the darkness of night the evidence of the crime committed to the earth. But one of the murderers, haunted by his crimes, fled first from one place, then from another; and the war in the Punjaub then being in progress, enlisted, as he said, in the hope of being killed in battle. By the time he joined his regiment the first Sikh campaign had been brought to an end. For some time he was therefore obliged to undergo the monotonous routine of regimental duty in an Indian cantonment, brooding in secrecy over the one terrible crime he dared not confess. At last the second Sikh war broke out, and when the 3rd Dragoons came in contact with the enemy he rushed desperately on with no other object than meeting death. But he was foiled, and after a couple more years of dull monotony and brooding over his own secret, he determined to strike an officer, in order, as he hoped, to be tried and shot for the offence, as a soldier of the 14th Light Dragoons had shortly before been at

Meerut, for a similar crime. All these particulars were carefully reported by me in the proceedings of the Board at the time. The 3rd, being ordered home, however, left the station, this man accompanying the corps, and I heard nothing more of the man till 1868, when, having to visit the regiment officially at Chichester, prior to its embarkation for another term of Indian service, I inquired after Brown of the one only officer who then remained of those who had left Wuzzeerabad with it. He informed me that the account given by Brown had been verified on their return to England, but that the man himself had become a confirmed lunatic, and had been sent to an asylum. I am induced to give the narrative as illustrating one phase of life in those who join the ranks of the army.

It would be foreign to the objects of these papers to discuss the probable occurrence of what is callèd *moral insanity* among the different members of a regiment in India. That such a form of mental affection does exist, however, is undeniable, although the line of demarkation between it and ill-regulated passion or vice is so imperfectly defined that it is difficult, nay, often impossible to say at what precise point the one ceases and the other begins. There is, however, much reason to believe that were the views held by authorities in the laws in regard to this important question more in accordance than they are with the truths exhibited by medical investigation, many of the breaches of military discipline committed by soldiers, instead of being, as they so frequently are, visited by heavy sentences, would be looked upon as manifestations of moral infirmity, as much as an ordinary injury or disease is of the physical system, and would be treated accordingly. There is much reason to believe that the mental faculties of both officers and men serving in India, are in a higher state of *exaltation* than of those who reside in more temperate climates. Hence, perhaps, the tendency so general in that country of magnifying the importance of derelictions of duty, and of the more venial offences so often observable there ; and hence it may be assumed many of the scandals and acts of tyranny which far too often are recorded in the local papers, or form subjects for the different law-courts there and at home. This branch of my subject is a fertile one, but it may be advisable merely to observe that nowhere more than in India, if indeed anywhere so much as in that country, does the remark hold good, that the subjects of passion, rage, and various forms of mind, are quite as often suitable objects of medical treatment, rather than for the military ordeals, which literally serve to aggravate rather than relieve the *disease* under which they labour. The older I become, the more leniently I feel inclined to look upon many *crimes* committed by men of long Indian service, and of those who have suffered from bodily ill-health there.

The affection known as *nostalgia*, or *home sickness*, which in former years was of frequent occurrence in the army, seems in more recent times to have ceased among soldiers. Probably, the altered conditions of service now as in former times have been the cause of this difference, and, if such be the case, the circumstance speaks more than almost any other in favour of the many improvements that have, during the last thirty years, taken place in the condition of the soldier. I may observe that these remarks are meant only to apply to what may be called idiopathic cases of nostalgia, or those in which, without the preseuce of any physical disease, the person becomes seized with a longing to return to his former home and friends, so intense as to amount to a form of monomania. Such a condition is by no means rare during the course of severe or tedious bodily illness, and has an important bearing upon the best manner of disposing of such men with a view to their convalescence and recovery. There are few, if, indeed, any, medical officers in India, who have not been appealed to by soldiers against the proposal to send them to a hill "sanatorium;" these were often declaring that if they could not be sent home to their own country they would prefer remaining among their own regimental acquaintances to being sent anywhere else, and the surgeon of experience never failed to have due regard to the wishes of the man, knowing as he did that his acquiescence or refusal would exercise the effect of, it may be, restoring in a great measure the hopes and strength of the patient, or of consigning him to a weary and desponding period of illness, too often to be ended only by death. This question has an important bearing upon that of having sanatoria for our Indian troops at the Cape, Australia, and elsewhere, in preference to sending them home. I would not now discuss it farther than to observe that I myself have heard sick soldiers declare that if they could not be sent home they would prefer being left to die as and where they were, that one foreign country was the same to them as another, and all they cared for was to get home, meaning thereby to the United Kingdom. While upon this subject I may also observe, that so far as my experience enables me to state, soldiers are, as a body, indifferent to the physical fact of dying. In my regimental career I have only in one instance been asked by a sick soldier as to my opinion of his illness, although I have necessarily come in contact with men of almost all positions of life, education, and characters.

Delirium Tremens.—The published statistics of delirium tremens indicate a difference in the rate of mortality by the disease at different stations in India, and in different years, so great, that it is difficult to assign a satisfactory explanation of the circumstance. It might have been suspected that medical officers did not always include the same conditions in their nomenclature; thus, an attack which one would designate delirium tremens, another would record under the head of "ebriositas," or "alcoholismus," or "febris à potu," and *vice versâ*; yet this is scarcely sufficient to account in all cases for the difference alluded to, which has been found to oscillate between 5 and 16 per 100 treated, or even more. According to the records of the 10th Foot, 48 soldiers were treated for this affection, and 34 for "ebriositas," of which numbers, 8 of the former, and 3 of the latter died; two officers had delirium tremens, both recovering, and with regret it must be said, that the wife of a soldier had so bad an attack, that her death released her husband of her. Four others appear to have been treated for "ebriositas," all of which particulars are very sad no doubt, and not by any means calculated to raise our estimate of such representatives of the *gentler* sex.

The young medical officer is scarcely prepared to find that the larger number of admissions by delirium tremens, instead of happening, as he would have expected, among the notoriously dissolute soldiers, occur in those who have an excellent *military* character, and are probably in possession of *good conduct badges*; a little experience, however, teaches him, that although the ill-regulated outbursts of the latter class often involve themselves *in trouble*, it is only among the former that the steady *boozing* goes on, which saturates the system, and too surely ends in some one of several dangerous diseases, among which that now being considered is one.

Among the habitually drunken, an attack of the affection is very liable to occur, on the receipt by them of an injury demanding their admission into hospital. A similar tendency is always noted in civil life, but in military, and especially in the case of an officer, the circumstance should be borne in mind, as it may have an important bearing in the evidence that may be demanded of a medical officer before a tribunal of justice. In such a case the immediate cause of the attack may be the "shock" of the injury itself, to a constitution already deranged by a state of alcoholism, while in others, in which the hurt is of trivial severity, it can only be attributed to the circumstance of the patient being for a time, whether by accident or on purpose, deprived of his habitual stimulus. Many cases of this kind occur in the experience of all regimental surgeons, and it is more with a view to illustrate the military bearing they may have, than any purely medical point, that I here allude to a small episode which once occurred to myself in reference to a case of this description:—In 1854, while stationed at Meean Meer, I received an order from the officer commanding the regiment, directing me, on the discharge from hospital of any soldier whose illness had been induced by "drink," to send to the orderly-room a special report on his case. Shortly afterwards, an old soldier, known as a regular "toper," having accidentally sprained his ankle, was admitted into the ward, where, in the course of a few days, partly no doubt from the shock of the injury itself, partly from the circumstance of enforced abstinence from his habitual stimulant, he became the subject of delirium tremens. In due course, he recovered from the effects of his accident, and also from the disease which supervened, and was discharged to duty; the report called for not being transmitted—whether through inadvertence, or, because the case was not considered to come within the category described, I do not now remember; nor does it materially signify. The omission, however, was speedily taken notice of, and I was called upon for my reasons in writing for having failed to obey the orders communicated to me by the commanding officer in regard to the reports already alluded to, with especial reference to this particular case, notwithstanding that, as stated in the letter addressed to me on the subject, it was stated that "the illness of Private So-and-so was clearly the result of drink." Had it not appeared to me, that a desire existed to take advantage of what could only be looked upon as a small matter, my reply might have been different from what it was. As it was, however, I confess I took advantage of a point, in which a similar opportunity will always be afforded when men, whether officers or others, write on matters beyond their own sphere of knowledge. In this instance a *military* officer had expressed his views in regard to the causation of a particular disease, and, as a matter of course, afforded an opportunity to me, of which, under the circumstances, I availed myself. The actual cause of the attack had not been "drink," but the fact of the man having had to cease drinking. No doubt, if he had not in the first instance been addicted to the vice, no mischief would have arisen from his enforced temperance; but as at the time this small incident occasioned a good deal of comment in regimental circles in the vicinity, as well as personal unpleasantness, I briefly mention it here as an illustration of what probably has occurred to many surgeons of regiments in India, where official correspondence is often conducted with a degree of asperity that can only be accounted for by that state of *nervous exaltation* to which I have already alluded.

That the person who has had one attack of this disease is thereby rendered more liable to a second, and so on, is sufficiently well known in a regiment, while it would also appear that the more frequent the attacks, the smaller is the amount of indulgence required to ensure another. As to the precise manner in which an attack supervenes, it may do so in one of two ways. For example: an old soldier, who for years has led a dissipated life, "goes on the spree," as it is called in the slang of the barracks. He abandons himself to intoxication and passion. At last his indulgence palls upon him, and he is forced to desist from his saturnalia through sheer inability to further continue them. But it is impossible, while ceasing his so-called indulgence, to emancipate himself from the effects of his orgies. He has had insufficient and broken sleep; he desires to have long and sound rest. He has had insufficient and probably unwholesome food. He finds he cannot, when he would, retire to sleep; nor is he able to enjoy wholesome meals when placed before him. His whole functions are deranged, and possibly remorse adds its depressing effects to the causes of his physical depression, and he passes into a state of "horrors"—he becomes the subject of delirium tremens.

Another, perhaps a younger soldier, is, from some accidental circumstance, betrayed, as it were, into a "bout" of dissipation. Having once passed the limits of self-control, he drinks fast and deep. Meantime he knows he has committed himself; he becomes desperate. If a non-commissioned officer, he perhaps squanders the money committed to his charge by his captain for the payment of his company; dismay follows; and what between the effects of his dissipation on the one hand, and remorse on the other, an attack of delirium tremens, probably with homicidal monomania, follows.

The disease is characterized from the earliest stages by extreme restlessness on the part of the patient; his movements are hurried and excited. The mind is more or less affected: in the slighter forms, probably in regard to matters connected with his daily occupations, but in the more severe cases, the hallucinations are of the most frightful character, from which circumstance the disease has obtained among soldiers the very appropriate name of "the horrors." A common form of delusion is that a conspiracy exists against the life of the person, that he is about to be tried by court-martial for some heinous offence, or that, having been tried he has been sentenced to be shot if a soldier, or perhaps to be cashiered if an officer. At other times he is haunted by phantoms of all degrees of horror, these taking in some instances their character from the nature of the religious views entertained by him; and not unfrequently under these he watches his opportunity to commit self-destruction; while in still another class of cases the person affected seeks for the opportunity, not to take his own life, but that of some one else, for which purpose he secretes about his person whatever weapon or other instrument he can become possessed of. In the early years of my military experience I met with an example of each of these forms, and the impression produced by them at the time has never been effaced. In one, the patient, an old soldier of *the Buffs*, stationed at Allahabad in 1844, was admitted into the regimental hospital, suffering under a very aggravated attack of the disease. He believed himself to be haunted by phantoms of the most horrible description. For several days and nights, notwithstanding the administration of the remedies usually given in such cases, he continued without sleep, restless, and tormented by demoniacal hallucinations. At last he fell asleep, and it was hoped that his malady was about to give way to the treatment employed. This hope was, however, soon dispelled. Shortly after he had fallen into the deceptive slumber, he suddenly sat up in bed, his features expressive of the utmost horror and alarm. He screamed for the hospital sergeant, who, at the time, was near, to save him from the devil, who, he asserted, had already got hold of him; and, falling back in convulsions, speedily expired. In the other case which I would cite as an illustration of the affection, the patient had apparently determined to take the life of his medical officer, for which purpose he had laid his plans with considerable ingenuity, and secreted one of the hospital knives, not altogether unknown to the warders placed over him, although neither had the determination to obtain possession of it from him. When, after these arrangements had been made, I paid the ordinary visit, he, in a confidential manner, expressed his desire to speak to me *alone* in an adjoining room, which was at the time unoccupied. I, as a matter of course, accompanied him, but, when in the act of entering, was made aware of my position by one of the attendants whispering into my ear, "Take care, sir; he has a knife concealed about him." As, however, my only reason for mentioning the circumstance here is to illustrate what are the "experiences" of regimental medical officers in India, I would merely observe that by the exercise of a little resolution, and, at the time, self-possession, personal risk was averted, and the subject of homicidal monomania disarmed.

The following cases illustrate some of the phenomena of the disease as usually observed in India, and the treatment usually adopted at the dates to which my notes refer.

—— McC., an officer of the 87th Regiment, was seen by me in April, 1852, at Wuzzeerabad, in the Punjab, suffering from what he himself called "the shakes"—the effect of hard drinking. He had but just arrived at that place from Ferozepore, having travelled the whole distance from Lahore—that is, upwards of 70 miles—on horseback. He stated that he had not been sober for six months; that he felt desirous to sleep; and that if he could but get sleep, he knew he would be all right. His manner was at this time restless, his skin cool and covered with perspiration, pulse slow, hands and tongue tremulous, the latter coated with fur, the bowels constipated. Forty drops of tincture of opium in a glass of beer were immediately given, and in the course of the evening, and shortly after the administration of the dose, he fell asleep. It was hoped that his threatened attack had been warded off, but in the course of the night he rushed suddenly into the bedroom of an officer whom he had come to visit, and in whose house he was, appearing at the time in great alarm, as he said that some person had just entered his apartment to do him bodily injury. I saw him soon after this. It was apparent that the dreaded attack had supervened. His pupils were now contracted; at one time he was under the belief that he was about to be shot; at another, that snakes, scorpions, and *devils* were under his bed; and then again, that his mother and sisters were dancing upon the surface of the wall. Five grains of opium were now given, and repeated every half-hour until six doses had been administered, he being allowed to have beer, brandy-and-water, and champagne, as he asked for each, but in moderate quantities with reference to his condition and habits. Sleep was not produced. His hallucinations continued, although he was readily pacified. His bowels remaining inactive, a moderate dose of croton oil in combination with tartarized antimony was given, and, no effect being produced, it was, after an interval, repeated; a moderate evacuation resulted; yet still there was no sleep. Tincture of opium was now given largely in beer, a blister applied to the nape, and the vesicated surface dressed with powder of opium. The dose of laudanum was repeated from time to time, until he had taken in all *three* ounces of laudanum, in addition to the opium administered in other ways : still no sleep was obtained, and the delirium had become aggravated. It was feared that to continue the administration of opium alone would be to incur the risk of poisoning by that drug ; a blister was accordingly applied to the scalp ; croton oil combined with two grains of the powder of opium and two of extract of colocynth, were given every two hours, until his bowels were freely evacuated ; and soon after they had been so, he fell asleep, on the afternoon of the third day after I had first seen him. He continued to sleep soundly till the forenoon of the following day. On awaking he was somewhat incoherent, but in every respect much improved. He had a chop and beer, and, in the course of the afternoon, was so much improved, that he expressed himself "all right now." His recovery was from that time rapid and continuous.

—— Buckley, 10th Foot, twenty-nine years of age, ten years in India, had been admitted a few days before the 16th November, 1858, on account of gonorrhœa. On that day symptoms of delirium tremens presented themselves, for which he was treated by a dose of calomel and jalap, followed by forty drops of tincture of opium in beer. On the 17th the attack had become more defined ; he was at times violent, and showed a desire to throw himself down a well in the hospital enclosure. A drachm of laudanum was administered every two hours, each dose containing half a grain of tartrate of antimony ; a blister was applied to the nape. Towards the afternoon of the 18th he fell asleep, and so continued till the morning of the 19th, when, on waking, he appeared quite rational and in all respects well. He had taken nine drachms of tincture of opium, and was now ordered to have chops and beer.

NEURALGIC AFFECTIONS.

Various forms of the maladies comprised under this head are met with in regimental practice in India, some being among the ordinary results of long residence in that country. Women were, until recently, believed to be more liable to this class of diseases than men, and there are many circumstances connected with their conditions, which, in a measure, would account for their being so. I find, however, that lately, it has been asserted by authorities in military medicine that the converse is the case: that these diseases more frequently affect men than women. Of course the statistics of one regiment are by themselves insufficient to decide such a question. They nevertheless have a certain value, and therefore I note that in the 10th Foot their rate of occurrence was 0·69 per cent. of strength among soldiers, 10 among their wives, 1·71 among officers, while, as might have been expected, children were altogether exempt. Here, then, we observe a very remarkable liability of the officers, as compared with the other classes noted, to attacks of neuralgia.

It is, unfortunately, now impracticable to record definite information in regard to the precise seat of the affection usually designated "neuralgia," as observed in India at the time referred to in these notes; but there is every reason to believe that *sciatica* is that most frequently indicated—a disease which, as will hereafter be more definitely indicated, as sometimes occurring in connection with the diffuse muscular rheumatism, which forms a frequent sequence of fever, at others, as a direct effect of malarious influences to which its subject has been exposed for a greater or less time. Another prevalent affection of this nature attacks the facial, frontal, or occipital nerves; the agonies of its paroxysms being, under certain circumstances, so severe as to render the existence of the patient one of continued misery. Many cases of this form occurred as a sequence of intermittent fever, which, as already recorded, prevailed at Wuzzeerabad as an epidemic in 1850-51, the general health of the patient sympathizing with, and becoming impaired, in proportion to the continuance of this affection. Another form of disease included under the same general head was vertigo, or giddiness, arising, no doubt, as it often did, from mere impaired physical powers, such as is frequently observed in persons who have spent several years in India; in others, as a result of long exposure to direct solar influences; and in a third class of cases, following upon previous attacks of such diseases as are ordinarily endemic in the country.

Of the pathological conditions upon which neuralgia depends, no definite knowledge was obtained at the time to which these notes refer. The affection was looked upon as entirely of a functional nature, and one of the many effects of malaria, all of which expressions are but indications that the precise conditions which accompany an attack of the kind were as yet unrecognized. I would observe, however, that while preparing my notes for the press, a new light is thrown upon this subject by Professor Rolleston. He gives expression, before the British Medical Association, to the views of Niemeyer, Dubois-Reymond, and Mollendorff, that the causation of certain forms of neuralgia is to be found in the fact of the dilatation and distension of the vessels supplying the affected twigs with blood,—a theory regarding which it is only necessary to observe in this place, that, for all practical purposes, it leaves the subject very much as it was. Supposing that these conditions do actually produce intense pain in the twig affected,—what then? We are no nearer a correct theory as to the appropriate means for preventing or removing such a condition than we were before.

In all the cases of these affections which came under observation, tonics and anodynes were the remedies usually employed; but in none can it be said that a permanent, beneficial effect was produced by medical treatment. It is true that in many instances temporary relief was obtained from the local application of the oil of the *Melaluca Cajeputi N. O. Myrtaceæ*—a native remedy; but this is one of the many affections incidental to foreigners in India, from which permanent relief is only to be obtained by complete removal from the conditions under which the malady was contracted, as to the hills or to England, while, in not a few, attacks continue to recur for years, if, indeed, not ever afterwards, even under the latter favourable circumstances.

Hydrophobia.—I may, in this place, offer a very few observations on that terrible disease, hydrophobia, an affection which, although the direct result of an animal poison being introduced into the system, so much so as to make poisoning, *necusia*, malignant pustule, and others which could be named, may, nevertheless, be considered as especially affecting the nervous system of the sufferer from it.

When the fearful extent to which rabies prevails among the pariah dogs that infest native villages in India is considered, and the number of natives who suffer from the terrible effects of their bites, it seems somewhat strange, but at the same time is a most fortunate circumstance, that during thirteen years my late regiment was in India, only one case occurred in it. The pathological condition upon which hydrophobia depends being so obscure, I give the following verbatim from the Annual Report, although, in itself, it possesses nothing of unusual interest; yet, every case ought to be carefully noted. "A well-marked and fatal case of hydrophobia has to be recorded (1847-8) at Lahore)." The subject of it was a patient under treatment for fever, who had been bitten in one of his fingers three weeks previous to admission. He was suddenly seized with a few anomalous symptoms; with a suffocating sensation of the throat, and general spasmodic action of the muscles supervened, together with the characteristic symptoms of the disease, namely, dread of fluids. He sank under these dreadful symptoms in the course of twenty-four hours from the commencement.

The wound from the bite of the dog had quite cicatrized. The post-mortem examination in this case revealed no other appearance that could be termed morbid, than a slight turgescence and vascularity of the mucous lining of the stomach and intestines.

I may remark that since the above notes were first written, I have seen two cases of this fearful affliction, namely, one in the person of a Chinaman, another in a Hindoo, and in both the futility of medical treatment was rendered but too apparent. Hemp, opium, chloroform, hot applications, cold applications, in fact, every variety of means were tried but without avail, relief being only obtained in the supervention of that unconsciousness which preceded death.

Cholera.—The notes upon which my present observations are based, range at intervals from 1841 to 1867. Some refer to actual personal experience, some to cases casually seen in course of inspectorial duties, while others are the result of perusing official documents, as well as the works of army surgeons who are, from their position, capable of expressing themselves with some degree of authority upon the subject. I am well aware that of late years the phenomena of cholera and the laws according to which it would appear to be regulated have been investigated with a degree of care and by the aid of scientific appliances unattainable at the time to which my earlier observations refer; yet, how far knowledge in regard to these two important points has been advanced beyond the point at which it then stood is a question, the solution of which must, I fear, be left to individual thinkers.

With these preliminary remarks I would observe that, like all other medical officers who have been some years in India, two forms of the disease have come under my notice, namely, the asphyxiated and the spasmodic. The former is of comparatively unfrequent occurrence, but its attack is, in the great majority of instances, fatal; the latter is the form which usually prevails epidemically, and although it also is unfortunately fatal in a ratio almost beyond any other disease which now affects our troops in India, it nevertheless leaves room for treatment, and affords recoveries in so many cases, even of the most desperate nature, as to encourage us in continuing our remedies when their use is based upon scientific principles. These two forms are not recorded separately in statistics of regiments, so that it is impracticable to state the actual ratio in which they respectively occur, neither am I now in a position to represent in figures the precise extent of, and mortality among, the various classes of persons borne upon a regimental establishment. In the records of the 10th Foot, however, I find accounts of 162 cases as treated from time to time. Of these, 85 were fatal among the soldiers, giving a ratio of mortality of 52·46 per cent.; of three officers attacked, all died; of 24 women 17 succumbed, or 76·83 per cent.; and of 10 children attacked, 8 died, or a ratio of 80 per cent. In some of these instances the disease attacked isolated individuals, but in the great majority it prevailed in epidemic form, and when it did so its rate of mortality was greater than under the former circumstance.*

The records of the regiment clearly show that the disease prevailed most extensively and severely during the first four years of its Indian service. The actual cases of the malady are stated to have been on an average 120 per annum during that period, the average yearly number for the subsequent nine years being 43. These facts are quite in accord with what has been noted by other observers, for it is now acknowledged that although the danger is undoubtedly great of cholera appearing in a regiment during the earlier period of its Indian service, yet epidemics of this disease often occur in what used to be called *seasoned* corps as well as individuals; that in the case of persons their greatest liability to such attack is first in the early period of their residence in the country, and again when

---

* See also a paper on this disease by the present writer, *Med. Times and Gazette*, Nov. 22, 1856.

they have spent many years in its exhausting and *malarious* climate.

As to the precise nature of cholera, or of the influence upon which the disease primarily depends, it may, I think, be confidently asserted that, notwithstanding all the care and scientific acquirements of the able men who have set themselves to the investigation of this point, our actual stock of definite knowledge regarding it is little if at all more satisfactory than it was many years ago. True it is that we may be upon the threshold of discovery, yet the condition as at present existing is as I have stated, and I much mistake if some of the remarks on the disease published in 1846* are not quite as applicable now in 1870 as they were when first written. At that time I had witnessed two outbreaks of the disease in India, namely, one in the Buffs in 1843, while the regiment occupied the fort of Allahabad, and again the following year on the return of the corps to that station after the campaign against Gwalior. I then observed that were the question asked What is cholera? nine-tenths of the Profession would answer, and correctly, "I do not know." "All we do know is, that the disease is generally attended by profuse vomiting and purging of a clear liquid resembling rice water; and from the immense quantities evacuated we can only account for its generation by supposing it to be the serum of the blood, of which there is hæmorrhage going on from the inner surface of the stomach and bowels." Can it yet be asserted that, as regards true knowledge of this subject, we are in a better position than we then were? Nor is it in regard to cholera alone that a similar remark is applicable. In the great majority of *morbid* conditions, and in the ordinary manifestations of the *vital* functions, we are accustomed to observe definite processes as taking place, but when we endeavour to trace them back to their ultimate causes we speedily find ourselves dealing with mere abstractions. This fact must be familiar to all who

---

* Principal Diseases of India. Published by Trelawny Saunders.

have endeavoured to trace up the causation of disease to its primary source, and, therefore, I need now only remark that we are probably neither in a worse nor better position in regard to our theories as to the origin of cholera than we are of many other diseases which we are accustomed to speak of as depending upon *malaria*, climatorial influences, epidemic influences, septic conditions, and so on. What really are all such terms but mere abstract expressions?

An attempt has indeed been made to define the actual influence upon which the disease cholera depends, but it is almost needless to observe the definition has merely resolved itself into words; the actual conditions have not been demonstrated. Thus we read in one place the actual cause described as consisting of an unknown something the essentials for the development of which include 1. The cholera miasm; 2. Humidity, and 3. The prevailing wind; that it is earth born and air conveyed; again, that the cholera germs lie hidden in the ground, that occasionally they are extricated in sufficient quantity to develope a few cases of the disease, and that when the atmospheric condition, including air and water, is favourable to the *cholera seed*, the disease becomes developed in its full vitality. These are indeed not the actual words employed by some modern writers on the subject, but they indicate the purport of speculations intended to take the place of established facts.

It is true that of late years various circumstances have been observed which would seem to indicate that an alliance of no distant kind exists between cholera and certain forms of fever. In reports of medical officers stationed at Peshawur, I, on many occasions between 1862 and 1867, observed remarks to the effect that such apparent alliance between cholera and intermittent fever had been suspected by them; that, in fact, in many instances, it was not possible in the very early stages of the attack to prognosticate whether the symptoms were those of cholera or of the severe form of ague prevalent in that insalubrious valley ; at Calcutta I have had occasion to observe a similar circumstance, and statistics prove that epidemics of cholera are in many instances followed by epidemics of fever. Medical officers who have served in the West Indies as well as in India, have, moreover, remarked that in not a few cases the character of the disease reminds them much of what they had observed in yellow fever. I have myself seen two cases in which this was particularly apparent, namely, one that of an officer in Calcutta, and a second in the person of a soldier at Tientsin in China. In both, *black* vomit was unequivocally present, and in both the attack was rapidly fatal. May I also refer to my papers on "Army Surgeons,"* in the *Medical Mirror* for 1868-69, for further evidence as to the supposed relationship of these two terrible forms of disease? These circumstances may no doubt indicate the fact, so often expressed by army surgeons, that geographical position and conditions connected with physical geography, climate, &c., modify the phenomena produced by similar causes, but they do not enable us to arrive at any more definite views than we already entertained as to the ultimate nature of that cause.

Adverting to the manner in which the disease makes its attack and is propagated, the experience of our army medical officers is very much in accord. They know that the disease may and does prevail, not only in different parts of India, but in the same stations at different periods of the year, and that in the great majority of instances the outbreak of an epidemic is preceded by a marked prevalence among the soldiers of diarrhœa, although there are exceptions to this rule. The results obtained from a study of the records of the 10th Foot are quite in accord with general experience that the disease usually begins in Bengal during the earlier part of the year, and gradually travels from that point towards the north-west. They

* Published separately by Lewis of Gower street.

moreover indicate that the course of the epidemic is not under all circumstances thus regular. For example, in 1845, when cholera occurred and prevailed fatally in that corps and the 9th Lancers at Meerut in 1845, the epidemic without doubt reached that station from the westward. In confirmation of the view that the disease does not in all cases occur in the North-west Provinces as an extension of the disease from Lower Bengal, I would refer to what Dr. Macpherson * says on this subject. He believes the common notion to this effect to be groundless, and the importance in regard to the disease attached to the Gangetic valley to be quite exaggerated. Among other facts he mentions the occurrence of the disease among the pilgrims of Hurdwar in 1783 without any recorded connection with Bengal; that similarly in 1816, it occurred to all appearance, spontaneously among a tribe of gipsies halting at Sahibgunge; that in 1781 it was introduced into Bengal, having probably come down the Gangetic valley.

On more recent occasions its progress has been found to be irregular; the epidemic not only missing places in its onward progress, but actually doubling back upon itself as it were, and devastating those very stations or villages which it had at first spared. In other instances it has been found to spread in all directions from a place or a body of persons affected, as if from so many distinct foci, while in still another set of cases it has suddenly appeared at several places at great distances apart, the intervening towns and districts remaining free and throughout the season completely exempt from it.

Among other characteristics of the disease I may observe that outbreaks seem to have no reference to the prevalence of particular winds or "monsoons;" that cases do not occur continuously in barracks, houses in cantonment, or even in towns and districts; and that although in the great majority of instances communication can be traced between the affected and persons or places subject to the disease, yet it

---

* Cholera in the East.

is not always possible to establish any such connection. It is impossible to do so in what are called sporadic cases of the disease, and often in the case of ships in which it suddenly appears many days after being at sea.

Unquestionably, the malady in many instances seems to become localised in the most filthy part of cantonments and cities. This is not always the case, however, as illustrated during the attack among the Buffs at Allahabad, for at the very time the men of the 3rd Foot were severely visited by it, notwithstanding their being carefully managed as regards cleanliness and accommodation in barracks, the native inhabitants of the neighbouring dirty and crowded baazar were comparatively exempt.

A point of considerable importance in reference to the history of this disease is the fact that although the occurrence of accidental or sporadic cases is, in many instances, preliminary to an outbreak of the malady in epidemic form, yet they are not necessarily so ; while, on the other hand, an epidemic may suddenly burst upon a station or body of troops without the occurrence of any conditions to account for the circumstance. The most delicate chemical experiments have hitherto failed to detect any difference in the condition of the atmosphere on such occasions as compared with times when the disease is altogether absent, and the supposed prevalence of *fungi, blue mist,* and various other apocryphal existences must as yet be looked upon as constituting more a plausible and convenient theory than as established facts. We do know, however, that whether an epidemic attacks suddenly and unexpectedly, or advances steadily from more distant stations, whether preceded by diarrhœa or not, its greatest mortality takes place for the most part in its earliest period. It may disappear as suddenly as it occurred, or, according to a common expression, gradually expend itself ; it may continue onwards in a definite course, may as it were retrace its path as already mentioned, or seem to altogether disappear, either for that particular season or for several weeks. It has generally been considered that the occurrence of a thunderstorm such as are frequent in India conduces to the termination of an epidemic of this nature. No doubt such is the case in many instances, but that the rule is by no means invariable was proved on the occasion of the outbreak already mentioned as having taken place at Meerut in 1845. On that occasion the disease seemed to burst upon the station immediately after the occurrence of such a storm, and with this peculiarity, that its early violence fell more severely upon the officers and their families, than upon the soldiers and theirs. The commanding officer and the wife of the surgeon were among its earliest victims.

At the time to which my remarks chiefly refer, the number of stations occupied by British troops in India was far fewer than they have more recently been. The greater number of them were erected either on the banks of or adjoining the larger rivers, and then it was observed that this disease seemed also to travel along the course of those streams, although, perhaps, more frequently upwards than according to the current of them. It was, however, well known that the onward progress of an epidemic was interrupted by the occurrence of a river in its track, and that certain parts of a river's course seemed never to be free from the presence of this disease. Several years have now elapsed since it was customary to send our soldiers in country boats by river to the more inland stations, or down to Calcutta from them. Steamers with the large troop boats attached to them superseded the miserable boats in which soldiers were formerly transported, and steamers have now in their turn been surpassed by the railway. During the many years, however, that troops were conveyed in the manner first mentioned, medical officers in charge of them knew well that danger always existed. When the fleet had to "come to" for the night upon a low-lying shore several cases of cholera might, as a matter of course, be looked for, while there were particular tracts along the river course, in traversing which a more or less severe outbreak was tolerably certain to occur; yet in neither case did any circumstance present itself materially different from the ordinary conditions of the voyage. One well-known tract of this kind existed during several miles of the river course between Bhaugulpore and Monghyr. There the Ganges, which during the dry period of the year was scarcely a mile in breadth, became so large during the rains as to extend to a breadth of ten or even upwards. The district being not only very flat, but the soil of rich alluvium, tracts which, during the rainy season were completely submerged, were left uncovered during the dry seasons, and thus became prolific sources of emanations from organic matters deposited in and upon them ; but then again the same remark applies with more or less force to other portions, of the Gangetic valley, and hence, I fear are not here of themselves sufficient to account for the disease having domiciled itself at the places mentioned.

But there are certain localities distant from rivers where cholera is similarly domiciled—but such I am able to speak of from my own knowledge. It occurs at Raneegunge and from thence some distance along the grand trunk road, or, in other words, in the coal district there ; and there are probably readers of these pages who, when marching with troops by the road in question, have had painful experience of the circumstance. When a very few years ago the 55th Regiment landed in India, detachments as they disembarked, were sent by the road in question *en route* to Hazarabagh, and while on the march suffered very severely. from an outbreak of the disease which occured as each in succession arrived at Raneegunge, and clung to them during their earlier marches.

It has generally been considered, and I belive with good reason, that this disease is most prone to attack persons residing upon or near ground floors of houses in India. There may, however, be exceptions to this, the epidemic appearing under certain conditions to leap, as it were, over a wall, attacking the occupants of the upper story to the comparative safety of those below. Of this an illustration occurred in my own experience very lately. When in 1863 cholera prevailed at the military station of Benares, a building formerly used as a mint was by the Rajah of that place given over for occupation by a portion of the 20th Regiment, so as to reduce the numbers in barracks. This building consisted of two stories; an enclosure around it was bounded by a high wall, so as to cut it off from the adjoining native bazaar. The disease seemed to advance through the bazaar, and in its progress reached the building in question. Instead, however, of the men accommodated in the ground floor being the first attacked, those in the upper storey were so. In fact, I am under the impression that the latter altogether escaped, although upon this point I cannot now speak positively.

It almost amounts to a platitude to remark that among the circumstances which, under certain conditions, give rise to cholera, and localise the disease in particular places, defective conservancy arrangements and impure water are among the most constant and most important. The facts have come to be universally acknowledged; yet, according to practical experience in India, it is found that neither does cholera necessarily prevail with greatest intensity in the dirtiest parts of towns, nor is the disease at all times caused by the use of water holding decomposing organic matter in suspension. If we are to look upon the ultimate cause of the malady as an actually existing entity, dormant under certain conditions, but capable of being roused into activity under certain as yet undefined influences, we may in some measure be able to account for the first circumstance alluded to, and explain why, for example, the parts of Calcutta, and other native towns, in which filth of all kinds is permitted to lie festering in the streets, are less constantly the scenes of cholera than streets in which, by means of so-called "drains," matters of that description are allowed to remain stagnant at an inconsiderable depth from its surface, polluting the soil and producing emanations which become doubly pernicious by the obstruction thus placed against their free escape. In the one case, such emanations are no sooner formed than they are diluted and carried away by the winds, or by the rain, whereas, in the other, they probably undergo processes which increase their injurious properties ; thus it may be that persons residing immediately over or near an imperfectly constructed underground sewer become attacked by cholera, while those in the vicinity of more openly objectionable places escape. In the same way, a ready explanation presents itself of the little injury to health which occurred from the most offensive native habit, in the absence of public latrines, or other receptacles of filth, the residents of villages, and also of considerable towns, repairing to the outskirts in the early morning to perform their functions ; so also may we account for the absence of injurious results in China, from the custom adopted in that country of irrigating the growing crops with liquid ordure, while the presence of imperfect drains or soil otherwise saturated with animal matters, are frequently visited by outbreaks of this disease. In fact, it appears to me that in many cases the system of superficial drains for cantonments in India is for these reasons more suited to the conditions of the country than that of underground sewers, such as are being now recommended for adoption.

It will be in the recollection of some readers of these notes, that when, about 1850, barracks according to a new and improved plan were erected at Mean Meer, near Lahore, a system of cess-pit privies was at the same time instituted in connection with that portion of the station occupied by the infantry.

These pits were carried down to the water-bearing strata, and were about fifty-eight feet deep, the intention having been to permit their contents to accumulate. Two of them were only 118 feet from a well, and others not much more distant. The stratum at that depth consisted for the most part of a bed of sand through which water seemed to percolate readily, and when in 1853–4 the 10th Foot occupied the station, contamination of the water of those wells was suspected. The presence of the pits had also become objectionable from the offensive emanations which arose from them, and became disseminated along the barracks. I at that time protested strongly against them ; but not until eight years afterwards was any notice taken of my report on the subject, and then only when some of the evils I had predicted had actually happened ; thus in the Report of the Commission appointed to inquire into the circumstances attending the terrible epidemic of cholera by which that place and others were devastated in 1861, opinions and views that had long previously been expressed by me were quoted by the Commissioners. They noted my remark with regard to these pits full of abominations, that "the stench from them was at times perfectly overpowering." They then add, that "in their Annual Report for 1853–4, the Medical Board quoted the opinion of Dr. Gordon, of Her Majesty's 10th Foot, to the effect that this abominable system 'was calculated, in the course of a few years, to induce epidemics of cholera and fever.'" Two years afterwards, namely, in 1856, a severe attack of cholera occurred among the troops there, there having on that occasion been 495 cases and 265 deaths in a strength of 1,592 British soldiers. On the last named occasion, namely, in 1861, the water from the wells in question was examined by the chemist at Lahore, who expressed his opinion that "in some instances, at least, contamination had actually taken place ;" but in illustration of the remarks already made, it should be stated that although on the occasion of the great epidemic at Mean Meer the ravages of cholera were greatest in the 94th Regiment which occupied the barracks nearest to the cess-pits, and to the contaminated wells, yet the first outbreak of the disease did not take place there, but in the 51st Regiment, then occupying a part of the Artillery lines at the opposite end of the station, and at such a distance as to put all possibility of the water there being affected out of the question.

To summarise as briefly as possible some of the conditions under which cholera may occur, I would enumerate the following, namely :—

1. It may take place in isolated cases or localities.

2. In a succession of partial or local outbreaks.

3. In bursts of epidemic, devastating stations and districts in a definite course.

4. As similar bursts; but to leap, as it were, over places to attack those at a distance.

5. As affecting the occupants of certain parts of a town, station, or building, while others, apparently precisely similarly situated, escape.

6. From the operation of certain medicines, more especially drastic or saline purgatives, and from violent emetics.

7. In intermittent fevers, in some cases of dysentery, and in some other diseases.

8. In localities where it most constantly prevails endemically it less frequently occurs as an epidemic than it does in such as are at certain seasons completely exempt from it.

9. The presence of decomposing animal matter, more especially in the soil, as in cesspools, drains, cemeteries, &c., undoubtedly act under certain other conditions and at times as sources whence cholera may reasonably be believed to arise. At other times, and under other conditions, no such results occur from the presence of such matters.

10. Doubtless, water containing matter of cholera dejections, and that containing decomposing animal matters, frequently produces cholera in those who use it. It does not, however, do so invariably, or *necessarily;* and, as epidemics of the disease travel more frequently upwards along the course of the Ganges than downwards, the theory of water contamination is not sufficient by itself to account for the occurrence of the disease.

That cholera, in very many cases, utterly defies all treatment must, unfortunately be acknowledged; and, perhaps, this fact taken in connection with the terrible virulence with which, in the majority of instances, the first onslaught of the disease in epidemic form takes place may, in part, account for the little confidence felt by many persons in medicine in such cases, as well as the unscientific and empirical nostrums to which recourse has, in too many instances, been had, to the neglect of those principles of physiology and therapeutics according to which members of the medical profession usually treat maladies they are called upon to combat.

Of this want of success in the treatment of cholera non-professional men are not slow to take advantage, to the discredit of the science of medicine generally. This remark is simply illustrated in the report of the Commission regarding cholera in Northern India in 1861. In that report (page 251) we read that "almost every report of every medical officer tells the same story of hopeless failure in the attempt to combat the disease in its advanced stages;" that "not only did every remedy appear useless, but we have found a strong doubt prevailing in the minds of some of the most thoroughly competent of the medical officers whether the practical result of the existing systems of treatment has not sometimes been a positive aggravation of the mortality;" and again,—"In many instances (page 252) I imagine that the patient dies of the doctor rather than of the disease so long as we know nothing of the nature of the disease, and so long as we have the most opposite modes of treatment vaunted in their turns—how can it be otherwise?" and then they quote, exultingly, the remarks by Dr. Elliotson when treating of the disease in England. "If," said he, "all the patients had been left alone, the mortality would have been much the same as it has been."

It must, I fear, with deep regret, be acknowledged that these remarks have very considerable foundation. I could enumerate a variety of so called systems of treatment, and of individual empirical remedies, the *modus operandi* of which put all ordinary principles at defiance. For example I would allude to such measures as the injection of saline mixtures into the veins of persons affected with this painful malady to the neglect of all other means;

to the application of cauteries along each side of the spine from the nape to the sacrum, at the same time that the cravings of the patient for cold drinks were tantalised by the occasional exhibition of spoonsful of warm-water gruel. We next find that a plan was recommended of aggravating the vomiting, which is one of the most painful accompaniments of the disease, by the administration of large quantities of mustard : while some persons, acting apparently according to still more dangerous views, prescribed tartar emetic, as if with the object of accelerating the depression which the disease by itself was sufficient to increase to the utmost before death. Space will not permit me to enumerate all the methods of *treatment* that have been from time to time adopted in this disease. I may, however, mention the administration of Epsom salts and tartar emetic combined ; the free use of water internally, sometimes hot, sometimes cold ; the affusion of cold water, partially or to the whole body ; the complete withholding of all fluids ; the administration of such agents as carbonate of soda in five-grain doses at long intervals ; the employment of *jactitation* so as almost literally to *shake the life out* of the patient ; and, perhaps, most horrible of all, the application of mechanical means to prevent discharge of the intestinal flux. As a further illustration, I would mention the following case, which came under my notice as lately as 1866, in Calcutta :—

A soldier of the Rifle Brigade, then in Fort William, having been admitted into hospital suffering from intermittent fever, he, during an accession of the cold stage of that disease, passed into decided cholera, and was treated by a recently arrived assistant-surgeon, whose scientific acquirements were described as being of a very high order. On visiting the patient sometime afterwards, I found him approaching a state of collapse, *notwithstanding* that he had received the following treatment :—A scruple of calomel had been administered on the accession of the choleraic symptoms ; a bottle of champagne had then been given, after which he was treated by solution of permanganate of potass in frequently repeated doses. I remonstrated, but was informed that the object was to supply oxygen to the blood, that the solution when vomited by the patient was quite *brown*, indicating thereby that it had parted with a portion of its oxygen, which must thus have been supplied to the system. This method of treatment was changed on the spot, and the patient subsequently recovered ; but I look upon the case as illustrating the theoretical views according to which this formidable disease is, it is to be feared, in too many instances trifled with.

In alluding to some remedies used in accordance with more scientific principles than those above enumerated, I would specially refer to venesection, calomel, and opium.

At one time the employment of venesection when practicable, was in common use, and in some cases advantage seemed to be obtained from it ; as a rule, however, it was impossible to abstract blood, partly from the circumstance of the circulation being so much enfeebled, and partly from the condition of the blood itself, so that this method of treatment was set aside as untrustworthy. Calomel, it is almost needless to observe, was given alone as well as combined with opium, sometimes in large doses, sometimes in small, but always with the double object of acting as a sedative and stimulating the flow of bile. How far either effect was ever produced was doubtful many years ago, although probably Medical officers hesitated much before abandoning what was then the *orthodox* treatment, and more recent researches into the action of mercury tend to indicate that their doubts were well founded. So with opium : the necessity for, as well as benefit to be derived from its employment had been questioned. In 1843-4 it was found that among the men of the *Buffs* at Allahabad, *secondary* fever, or, in other words, cerebral affection supervened in every case in which it had been administered largely, the mortality from that complication being larger in proportion than during the primary attack. The use of opium was accordingly abandoned in the hospital under my charge, and with favourable results, nor was it again used by me in subsequent regimental practice in India.

In briefly narrating the treatment adopted for cholera in the *Buffs*, and in the 10th Foot, it may be well to allude to the theory according to which our remedial measures were directed. Whatever may have been the nature of the influence upon which the disease ultimately depended, the tendency of that influence acting upon the human body was to produce death ; but practical experience had shown that in those cases where the vital powers were maintained sufficiently long by the employment of artificial stimulants or other means, those powers recovered their natural condition—slowly, and probably with interruptions, yet to such an extent as to constitute recovery. Bearing the above indications in view then, the following routine was that pursued, namely :—

1. To relieve the nausea, vomiting, and sense of sinking which characterised the first onslaught of the attack, carminatives, stimulants and antispasmodics were administered, as for example, a combination of the ethers, aromatic ammonia, tinctures of capsicum, ginger, and so on ; sinapisms being meantime applied to the epigastrium. It is almost needless to observe that the earlier in the attack these remedies were employed, the greater was the chance of success, and that whenever the disease was prevalent, arrangements existed by which soldiers attacked in barracks might immediately obtain medicine of this description.

2. The intestinal flux being looked upon as a flow of serum, dependent upon causes affecting the system generally, we considered that this indication should best be met by remedies directed to support the general powers instead of by those of a more special nature, such as direct astringents. Those, therefore, which were applicable to the indications first enumerated were held to be so to this.

3. In those cases, and they are numerous, in which

vomiting is persistent, notwithstanding the use of remedies ordinarily employed, diluted prussic acid in combination with the remedies already mentioned, was followed by such favourable results as to justify a further trial being made of it. As an adjuvant, counterirritation was employed to the epigastrium, either by means of a blister, or by the instantaneous application of a cloth dipped in sufficiently hot water to produce vesication.

4. To maintain warmth of the body as far as practicable, hot bottles, protected by flannel, were applied wherever most required. The surface was wiped with soft cloths, and kept warm as far as possible; but, as is well known, the coldness of the body and limbs of a patient affected with cholera, and which seems to have no reference to the season of the year, or state of atmospheric temperature, is only checked when circulation begins to be re-established.

5. The spasms which pervade the limbs were usually met by frictions, or by "kneading" the parts most severely affected.

6. The intense thirst which attends the disease is perhaps best moderated by the administration of ice; by brandy and water, alone or in effervescence; while the same stimulant in sago, whether hot or cold, was in many instances rejected by the patients.

7. Regarding the suppression of urine which attends the disease, it was customary to look upon the cessation of that symptom as an indication that the functions of the organs were being restored by the treatment already mentioned.

I would further observe in this place that, after experience in the treatment of the disease had been gained, we learned that, although, as already stated, secondary fever almost to a certainty followed, after opium in large quantities had been administered, provided the patient survived the first onslaught of the malady, this complication, under certain conditions, also happened where no opium had been given. In either case the affection was preceded by the occurrence of constipation, and was most surely averted by the employment of carminative laxatives, more especially in the form of tincture.

It need hardly be repeated that my purpose is not to give a systematic treatise on cholera. All I aim at is to communicate such of the results of my own experience of the disease as are likely to be useful to other Medical officers, and with this view I would submit the following cases :—

Hally, 10th Foot, admitted at Dinapore on 22nd August, 1857, suffering from the ordinary symptoms of cholera, attributed by him to exposure and the *use of bad water* while employed against the rebel sepoys in the jungles of Jugdespore. The symptoms were of an aggravated kind, but had not passed into the stages of collapse. A draught, composed of aromatic spirit of ammonia and sulphuric ether, of each twenty drops, and ten drops of tincture of capsicum was administered, and repeated every half-hour. Vomiting being obstinate after several doses of the mixture had been given, three drops of medicinal hydrocyanic acid were added, and the whole given in ℥jss. of camphor mixture. Mustard was applied to the epigastrium, and hot sago with brandy given. This treatment was continued throughout the 23rd, during the night of which all the symptoms moderated except the vomiting, and it still continued obstinate. According to the morning report of the 24th, natural warmth of the body had been restored. On the 25th the report stated that the choleraic symptoms were disappearing; but that the patient experienced a feeling of "fulness in the head," for which a draught was administered, consisting of ʒj. of tincture of jalap, ℥ss. of confection of senna, carminatives being continued at intervals. The improvement in his condition continued until the night of the 17th, during which he began to come cold again. Stimuli were immediately given, and hot bottles applied to the hands and feet. Under this treatment the temperature became re-established, and improvement was steadily progressive, no further treatment being administered beyond tonics of gentian and quinine, the bowels being regulated by the laxative, as above. On September 7th he was discharged to duty, having been sixteen days in hospital.

Constable,? 10th Foot, æt. thirty-seven, sixteen years in India, admitted at Dinapore, 23rd August, 1857. Having the day previous returned from cantonments from service in Jugdespore jungles, where he had been much exposed to sun and rain, he was, at 3 a.m. of that day, suddenly aroused from sleep by severe griping and purging. At seven o'clock he was brought to hospital, and immediately received a carminative draught. His eyes were then sunken, the tongue cold, fingers somewhat corrugated; the early stage of cholera was distinctly marked, and a few minutes after his admission cramps in the abdomen and limbs had become intense. A synapism was now applied to the abdomen; hot brandy in igo was administered; aromatic spirits of ammonia and sulphuric ether, each 20 drops, with 10 drops of tincture of capsicums, were administered every half-hour. In two hours after treatment had been commenced the symptoms began to moderate, leaving only exhaustion. No other remedy than a continuance of the carminative was required, and recovery was rapid and complete.

With regard to the *post-mortem* appearances in cases of cholera, I would here transcribe what I had observed so long ago as 1843-4, in reference to epidemics of the disease which visited the *Buffs* stationed at Allahabad in each of those years. My remarks on that occasion were that "in examining the bodies of those who have died of cholera, we are struck with the absence of all appearances which, under ordinary circumstances, would account for death. We always find extensive congestion of the venous system, the right side of the heart being gorged with dark liquid blood; and, what is a remarkable feature in the disease is the total absence of those coagula in the heart, which are usually discovered after death from other diseases. The stomach and bowels are remarkably pale; their inner surface coated with soft ropy matter, as if it had been smeared over with thick mucilage. The stomach usually contains a greater or smaller quantity of the medicines that had been administered in the course of treatment, and the lower part of the intestinal canal is filled with the characteristic rice-water fluid. The gall bladder is distended with dark ropy bile, and the urinary bladder is invariably contracted and empty.

The occurrence of increase of temperature in the bodies of those who die of cholera, and of spasmodic actions, both continuing for a considerable time after dissolution, are phenomena which, from their very nature, commanded the attention of Medical officers. They are by no means of invariable occurrence in those who die of cholera, nor are they confined to such, having been frequently noticed in the bodies of persons destroyed by yellow fever in the West Indies and South America ; but, when they are first observed, and especially if witnessed by a near relation of the deceased, the impression produced is something appalling. I give an example :—

Case of Lt. Followes, 53rd Regiment, Calcutta, 1856. About ten years ago, while stationed at Cawnpore, he had a severe attack of cholera, his recovery from which he attributed to having clandestinely drank nearly a bottle of brandy.

He ever afterwards retained a rooted fear and apprehension of the disease ; but his health continued good until the arrival of his regiment at Fort William, where, during the latter part of January and all February, 1856, he was frequently awakened suddenly at night by an attack of diarrhœa, attended by "spasms" in the abdomen. He never mentioned these to anyone but a servant, who used to procure hot water as a pediluvium, as well as some brandy and tincture of ginger, and under this treatment the symptoms disappeared.

On the 25th of February, 1856, he visited Dum Dum for the purpose of bringing back his wife, who was there on a visit. At breakfast he ate a large quantity of fruit, of which he was particularly fond, partaking, among others, of oranges and pineapple.

During the rest of that day he felt uncomfortable, but looked unusually well—so much so that his friends congratulated him. At dinner he had no appetite, and contented himself with a plate of soup. He complained of drowsiness, and during the meal nodded several times, although such was not his usual habit.

In the evening, when returning, he fell asleep shortly after entering the "garry;" but after a time awoke, feeling dreadfully sick, and with an inclination to be purged. He had to rush out almost instantly, when he vomited profusely, and had a copious alvine evacuation. His wife, on his return to his seat in the conveyance, having expressed her alarm and fear regarding his state, he said,—"Oh! there is no fear of me; I have once had cholera, and could tell at once if I had that disease."

He had no further evacuations previous to his arrival at his quarters about 10 o'clock (p.m.); yet, by that time he was so weak that he was unable to stand. From this time he was purged, and vomited six times before 3 a.m., cramps took place in his legs, the pain from which became intense. These extended to his stomach (abdomen) and loins. Jactitation was constant—he turned from side to side, tossed his arms about, and groaned from pain. His voice was hollow; his fingers corrugated; features sunken; a dark zone beneath the eyes; the tongue and breath cold; the pulse fluttering, and at times imperceptible; the entire surface bedewed with cold clammy perspiration, which stood upon his face in large prominent drops. The spasms continued a considerable time after both vomiting and purging had ceased; as the vital powers decreased his jactitation diminished, and then during each accession he could only moan, while, in subdued voice, he ejaculated, "Oh, God! Oh, God!"

About 4 o'clock, a.m., all bodily suffering ceased, and he fell into a deep sleep. The temperature of the surface now increased somewhat; the pulse beat more full and steady, and hopes were entertained that recovery might take place. Meantime, worn out with distress of mind and bodily exertion, his wife also dropped off in a slumber. About eight a.m. the pulse again began to flag—it rapidly sank, and then became imperceptible ; the warmth of surface gradually became less, and, without awakening him from his rest, he passed into death.

The widow awoke and looked calmly at the body of her husband as it still lay upon its side in the attitude of sleep.

She knew not the change that had taken place, neither could she realise its truth wheu informed of it—and now came a scene most trying and heart-rending. She rushed to the corpse, threw herself upon it, while she burst into an agony of tears and hysterical sobs. Sympathy at such a moment was out of the question, and she was left unmolested to give vent to her first burst of grief.

In a few minutes what was our horror to hear her scream—" Doctor, he moves, he moves ! " the last effort of muscular contractility showing itself in slight flexure of the fingers. In vain we endeavoured to convince her how delusive were her hopes of returning animation. But he's getting warm," she sobbed while she looked at us imploringly, " and must be alive." We had to point out that this peculiar phenomenon was also one of the fearful malady that had just claimed its victim.

It was difficult to form a theory capable of accounting for these phenomena, and I question if any satisfactory explanation has yet been given in regard to them. I will only quote the opinions of two eminent authorities :—Dr. Carpenter observes* that " Muscles possess the inherent property of contractility, yet are dependent upon the nerves for the exercise of that power." . . . . " This contractility may remain for some time after the nerves have ceased to be able to convey to them the effects of stimuli ;" and then goes on to remark that " whilst the

* "Human Physiology," pp. 391. et seq.

irritability of muscles is gradually departing after death, it not unfrequently shows itself under a peculiar form." . . . . "the most remarkable manifestations being witnessed after death from cholera and yellow fever, the muscular contractions in such cases being frequently spontaneous, and sometimes give rise to movements resembling the ordinary actions of the living state. Dr. Carpenter further quotes from Dr. Dowler, of New Orleans, various illustrative cases, in one of which this contractility continued upwards of four hours after death in a fatal case of yellow fever, in allusion to which it was remarked that many circumstances indicate that these movements were due to the inherent contractility of the muscles, and were not in any degree dependent upon the operation of the nervous system."

Referring to the increased bodily temperature after death in connection with *post-mortem* muscular contractility in these two forms of disease, he makes allusion* to the general fact, to which, however, there are numerous exceptions, that increase of bodily heat during life usually attends accelerated pulse, and decrease of temperature those affections in which the pulse is slow, although there are numerous exceptions. He observes that "it is not a little remarkable that the temperature of the body should sometimes rise considerably after death; and he gives a table, according to which it would appear that in some cases of disease the temperature of the thigh and epigastrium rose to 111° Fah. and 113° Fah., at the same time that the heat of the brain was only about 100°. He, however, gives no explanation of the phenomenon. He merely records it.

Professor Houghton would appear to be of opinion that the continuance of muscular motion and the occurrence of increased temperature after death "tend to prove that the impeded circulation, which is the prominent symptom in cholera collapse, is due to the constriction of the capillaries,

---

* *Op. cit.*, p. 638.

in consequence of which the muscles are deprived of their supply of freshly oxidised blood, the result of which is necessarily contraction and cramp, which produces the excessive agony and cramp that characterise the diseases."*

I regret much my inability to perceive that these observations contain anything approaching a sufficient explanation of the phenomena alluded to, and more especially of their occurrence, particularly in bodies of the dead, by only two diseases, namely, cholera and yellow fever. A similar increase of temperature is said to be sometimes observed in the bodies of those who die by tetanus.

The latest reference to this subject occurs in the *Lancet* of 1st January, 1870, where *post-mortem* temperature is briefly discussed. It is there stated that, respecting the cause of the phenomenon, one set of observers attribute it to *solidification* (rigidity of the muscles), others, to the continuance of *vital* action after the motion of the heart has ceased ; but it is apparent that neither of these *explanations* affords any real clue to the ultimate conditions upon which it depends. The subject, however, is one of great interets and importance, and will, it is hoped, be fully investigated.

There has of late years existed a manifest desire on the part of non-professional writers on cholera to rob Medical men, and more especially Army-Surgeons in India, of the credit justly due to them of having been the first to recommend measures for the prevention of this disease, which, although perhaps only partially acted upon when first recommended, have since been brought forward by so-called *Sanitary Reformers*, as if they were recent discoveries of their own. In the following remarks I desire to indicate some of the most important of the labours of Medical officers in reference to the sanitation of the disease, for which purpose I consider the subject in the following order—namely :

---

* Medicine in Modern Times, p. 144

(*a*) The origin and course of epidemics; (*b*) As to the probable dependence of the disease upon certain meteorological conditions; (*c*) Its probable connection or alliance with malarious diseases; (*d*) Its effects upon the prevalence of the ordinary endemic diseases; (*e*) Its connection with *epizootics;* (*f*) How affected by drunkenness; (*g*) Its favourite localities; (*h*) As to the correctness of nomenclature regarding it; (*i*) Means of prevention; and (*j*) Regarding isolation and removal of the infected.

a. Official records in the Army Medical Office, Calcutta, contain numerous observations which indicate that many years ago it was known that cholera usually, but not always, occurred first in Lower Bengal, and thence progressed to the more inland districts. In 1831, the Inspector-General in his "Annual Report"* records the circumstance that a case of this disease happened on the 6th of April among some men of the *Buffs* who were proceeding by the *Bhauguruttee* River from Chinsurah to Berhampore; that on the 16th of the same month it appeared among the troops at Chinsurah, at Dinapore on the 5th of May, Benares on the 8th, and Ghazepore on the 12th, so that although its progress seems to have been by a series of leaps rather than uninterruptedly onwards, its general course was upwards along the course of the Ganges. Two years afterwards, namely in 1833, Dr. Burke wrote that the disease "usually travels with the last windward rains, and is apparently arrested along with them." He moreover mentioned that "it seems to make its progress along the banks of the Ganges, spreading itself inland from these." Indeed, so well understood had the fact become in 1838 of the progress of the disease from East to West, and of its occurrence at particular stations at definite periods of the year, that any deviation from the rule became subject of remark. Thus it is said that since the beginning of that year "it had prevailed more

---

* Page 451.

extensively at Calcutta than is usual so early in the year."*

b. The fact that an outbreak of cholera is often checked by the occurrence of a thunder storm is generally recognised in India. It is alluded to in various official reports. It is stated to have had this effect when an epidemic of the disease, prevailed at Berhampore in 1829, and the circumstance is again alluded to in the Inspector-General's "Report" for 1835.† Unfortunately, however, this rule is not invariable. In 1845, cholera of a very fatal character occurred at Meerut among the 10th Regiment; and similar outbreaks after an unusual continuance of easterly winds, and after unusually heavy falls of rain, were not only commented upon before and shortly after that date, but formed the subject of investigation by the late Cholera Commission of 1861.

c. When in 1831 this disease prevailed in epidemic form at Ghazepore, the circumstance was mentioned by the Inspector-General in his "Report" for that year‡, that an increase in the severity of intermittent fever at the same station was observed; and with reference to the occurrence of a very fatal epidemic which raged in 1833, Dr. Burke expressed his belief that it appeared to have been caused by malaria.

Dr. McLeod observed in his report for 1835, that "on the disappearance of cholera, fever of the continued form began to prevail to a considerable extent among the young and robust, attended by severe headache and high arterial action. The tissues of the eye and the skin were usually of a yellow colour, but there were no other symptoms present to lead us to the conclusion of the liver being deeply affected." "Gastric derangement," he adds, "was a very common symptom." In the "General Report for India," for 1844, we find the following remarks relative to an epidemic of fever which had during that year prevailed

---

* "Report." 1836 to 1838.

† Page 324.

‡ Page 451.

in the 29th Foot at Ghazepore—"The pulse, almost always weak and frequent, about 100. In some cases the prostration was extreme from the commencement, *closely resembling the collapsed stage of cholera.* There was certainly a curious affinity between these two diseases—a livid colour of the skin, a turgidity of the lips and fingers in the severe cases of the epidemic."

The Surgeon of the *Buffs* thus wrote of the fever which severely affected the men of that regiment in 1841 :—" In several cases of remittent fever of the worst type pain was complained of, chiefly affecting the muscles, usually of the lower extremities. In several other instances when the patient was considered as going on favourably, the train of symptoms suddenly, and generally without any evident cause, underwent a most unfavourable change, assuming many of the features of cholera ; the extremities and body being icy cold, with feeble or no pulsation at the wrist, and scarcely any at the heart ; great prostration ; urgent calls for drink, frequently accompanied by muttering delirium." "These symptoms," Dr. Macqueen observed, "were more often observed in young men who had shortly before been in robust health ; and, it may be added, no recovery took place in such instances."

I would also observe that in and prior to 1831, Drs. Searle and Stevens suspected that an analogy existed between cholera in the East Indies and yellow fever in the West ; and that more recently, Medical officers, who have served and witnessed those diseases in both countries, have in their reports alluded to the same circumstauce in their phenomena.

d. A perusal of the reports on the state of regiments in Bengal for the years from 1826 to 1829, will suffice to indicate that Army Medical officers of that time were fully aware of the tendency which, during epidemics of cholera, the ordinary diseases of the country manifested to merge into that affection. Lest, however, I may be accused of simply dealing in generalities in this statement, I will give a definite instance: it occurs in the "Report" for

1829,* and there Dr. Burke expresses himself in this way. "Cholera," he writes, "like many epidemics whose history has been handed down to us, either modifies, changes, or, for a time, banishes the endemics of the season or country." And here I would allude to one lesson that is to be obtained from this brief paragraph. It is, that the Medical officers who wrote in 1829, were careful before expressing their own views to study the literature of the diseases regarding which it became their duty to write—an example I would strongly recommend for the adoption of some of their successors of the present time.

e. "It has often been observed," so wrote Dr. McLeod, "that during the prevalence of an endemial disease among the human species, the lower animals, and even fish generally participate more or less. This happened in a very remarkable degree in the month of March, 1829, when cholera morbus prevailed so extremely in the 49th Regiment, at the station of Berhampore in Bengal." He then goes on to advert to that epidemic, and thus continues: "It is a curious fact, and one worthy of record, that during the rage of cholera, a considerable number of fish of every sort and size to be met with in the large tank close to the barracks, sickened and died, or became perfectly powerless, floating on the surface of the water, so as to be easily caught by the natives." He further records the fact that "about the same time a distemper appeared among the dogs at the station, and prevailed to a great extent in a kennel of foxhounds," where it "carried off in a very short time the greater number attacked."†

f. I have already had occasion to allude to the evils which in India attend the distribution of money and bounty to soldiers, and especially to the drunkenness and riot which prevail at such times. Official reports inform us that under such circumstances cholera, in 1829,‡ broke out among the men of the 47th Regiment, then quartered

* Page 23.
† Report, 1835, page 317.
‡ Report, 1829, page 158.

at Berhampore, they having shortly before received their prize money for Ava, and that a similar occurrence took place at the same place among soldiers of the 14th Regiment after they had been paid their prize money for Bhurtpore. In the same year cholera, in epidemic form, attacked the men of the *Buffs*, stationed at Bhaugulpore, immediately on those who had volunteered from the 59th Regiment had received their prize money for Bhurtpore. We learn that much drunkenness prevailed there from the time those men joined the *Buffs*, and that the soldiers exposed themselves recklessly to the sun, roved about in search of liquor, and often bathed in the adjoining river, regardless of the dangers they thus incurred.

g. The great degree of liability of detachments of troops proceeding up by the river Ganges to be attacked by cholera, was noted so long ago as 1829.* Dr. Burke, in describing this occurrence, observes that "during an epidemic of the disease from which the *Buffs* suffered while travelling up by river route," and to which allusion has already been made, "the attacks were most severe when the boats remained during a night upon a low-lying muddy bank; and less so when under high and abrupt banks. Another circumstance recorded on the same occasion is not without its value now, namely, that the guard of natives attending the regiment suffered less from the prevailing disease than the soldiers.

The circumstance was also early noted that troops occupying ground floors of barracks were more susceptible of the disease than those upon upper storeys. Thus, on the occasion alluded to, when cholera occurred in the 49th Regiment at Berhampore, we are informed that "the soldiers and married families lodged in the lower floors were nearer to, and more intimately connected with the poison producing the disease" than those more elevated, "presuming," as the report goes on to observe, "that the poison emanates from the ground."† Another point connected

* Report, page 258.

† Report for 1829, page 156.

with this formidable disease, which we find alluded to in the older reports, is the liability of soldiers, while undergoing treatment in hospital, to become its subjects. This liability was specially alluded to in the report on the 49th Regiment, when, while quartered at Hazarabagh in 1838, the men of the corps became subjected to it, "a larger proportion of the men in hospital" being on that occasion seized with the disease, "than of those in barracks."

h. Some recent circumstances have induced writers to express an opinion that many cases which, in former days, were recorded as cholera, were not of such a degree of severity as to constitute what would now be only described as of that disease. It is argued, on the one hand, that the medical officers of the times to which in these notes I principally refer, were less cautious in the phraseology they employed in describing the disease than those of more recent days have become; and also that some, in order to demonstrate the success of particular modes of treatment advocated by themselves, were induced to include among their cases those that would not now be described as cholera.

That such imputations should be made without the most ample evidence that grounds exist for them, speaks little in favour of the medical officers who gave expression to them. Perhaps, however, it will be well if I, on this occasion, simply give a few references to what is recorded on these two points. With reference, then, to the question of nomenclature, we find Dr. Burke, in 1828, quoting from the report* of Dr. Sandham, of the 11th Light Dragoons, expressing himself to this effect :—"Every case attended with vomiting and purging should not be termed cholera, or, at all events, might sometimes have *modified* added to it." Again, the surgeon of the 44th Regiment, in his report for the same year,† makes the remark that "it is not his intention to insinuate aught against those who have boasted of their success in

* Report, 1828, page 195.

† General Report, 1828, page 226.

cholera, but he knows that none which were not indisputable cases of spasmodic cholera are entered under that head in his return."

These remarks, I submit, indisputably show us, that if in some instances there may have been a certain degree of want of precision in the application of the term "cholera," our superior medical officers, whether in departmental position or professional attainments, observed an amount of precision in the manner of applying the term not exceeded by their most advanced brethren of the present day.

And so also was it with the second class of cases to which I refer, namely, those where some medical officers, in order to magnify the success of particular modes of treatment, did not at all times observe strict care in designating as cases of cholera those to which the designation was really applicable. It may be assumed from the nature of the comments which I am about to quote that then, as in more recent times, the medical officers who wrote and spoke with the greatest amount of confidence of the success of their particular methods of treatment, were often those whose sphere of observation, and of action, was the most limited. It was of such that Dr. Sandham thus wrote, in 1828* :—"It is somewhat vexing," he remarked, "to see some speak so confidently, and who have seen but little of the disease, except among natives, in whom," he adds, "I have generally found it tractable enough." Dr. Sandham well knew what was wanting, in some cases, at least, in order to rectify the views of such medical officers. "The care of a very few Europeans would soon put them right." And, doubtless, so it would.

It is, in fact, tolerably clear that so long ago as the time to which I here refer, the impression had begun to be proved that the rates of mortality in outbreaks of cholera, were really much alike, whatever may have been

---

* General Report, 1828, page 195.

the plan of treatment followed, while the recorded success of some methods was probably more apparent than real. That this impression gained strength the longer the attention of superior medical officers was directed to it is apparent in the writings to which we have access; thus, for example, Dr. Clarke, when writing on the subject of cholera fifteen years afterwards, namely, in 1843, found himself driven to remark that "the ratio of deaths to recoveries from this terrible scourge cannot be estimated short of fifty per cent;" and, he adds—"I fear we must be compelled to acknowledge that little advance has been made in our treatment of this disease, from its first appearance in India to the present hour; certain forms of practice have been lauded as almost specific in their effects, which have been found, when employed afterwards during the period of the epidemic, totally unavailing."

i. Were we to believe what has of late years been said and written, we should be inclined to look with horror and contempt on the culpable ignorance displayed by our older army medical officers in regard to the precautions that were most likely to be successful against the onslaught of cholera. If, indeed, my readers have not already made up their minds on this subject—adverse, of course, to the claims of my departmental brethren—let me be permitted to solicit their attention to the following brief extracts from official reports which bear upon this question:—It is reported that so long ago as 1830,* "during the prevalence of cholera, health inspections of the troops were made twice daily, and no men were discharged from hospital until perfectly recovered." In 1833, again, it is stated that among the measures adopted to check the spread of the disease was this, that "the stuffing of the bedding of the patients in cholera was destroyed, the bedcases washed and fumigated, as likewise the store in which they were kept;" and we moreover find it stated that "after the first thirty cases, no

* Report for 1830, page 316.

bedding was served out to those admitted, except such as could be washed"—an arrangement, let us add, which, dictated in a parsimonious and unworthy spirit, inflicted much discomfort and personal injury upon the men who were subjected to it.

In this year also, Dr. Daunt, Surgeon of the 44th Foot, "did not fail to adopt every measure that might contribute to the prevention and extermination of the disease, as well as to the best mode of cure, and to the comfort of the sick." Among others adopted on this occasion, we learn that the barracks in which the disease appeared were successively vacated—"the walls thoroughly scraped, and the whole barracks thoroughly cleaned and whitewashed." It is moreover added that "if the season of the year had been favourable, an encampment at a distance from cantonments would have been recommended; but as it was, the weight of argument was considered to be against the arrangement."

The same series of reports informs us that, in 1835,* in addition to the personal inspection by the medical officers of the soldiers twice daily, as already described, "each non-commissioned officer received strict injunctions to watch the men of their respective companies closely, and to send them to hospital the instant they appeared to be in the slightest unwell;" and by those of 1836 we find it recorded that, on the occasion of the outbreak of the disease as an epidemic at Ghazeepore in that year, the system adopted was of "dealing openly and fairly with the men, by explaining to them the vital importance of attending to the first symptoms of indisposition, and pointing out to them, when they reported themselves early, the success with which they are treated, and the utterly hopeless condition of their situation when they have neglected these precautions, and been brought to hospital in a state of collapse;" and Dr. Burke, commenting on these arrangements, observes that "it is of the

* Report, 1835, page 331.

highest importance every soldier and officer should know that, however slight the case may appear at the first moment of attack, the progress is rapidly onwards to a state over which we have no power; and, on the other hand, that most cases where the early or premonitory symptoms are attended to, the disease is to be cured like any other."

j. Among the measures of late years proposed in outbreaks of cholera among troops, the separation of those affected with that disease from their comrades, the removal of the men affected to a greater or less distance from barracks, and their distribution in larger or smaller bodies have deservedly been considered as among the most effectual towards the prevention as well as extinction of the epidemic. It is something to know that the importance of these measures has been demonstrated to, and acknowledged by, non-professional men, and has been included among the steps which are now authoritatively ordered to be taken on occasions of epidemics of this nature. Those of my readers who are acquainted with what has been written on the subject of sickness in the West Indies, must be well aware that for generations back, isolation of men affected with yellow fever, and removal into camp of the men affected have been periodically put in force; but from some cause or another, there appears to exist, even among professional men, an imperfect knowledge of the extent to which similar arrangements were formerly made in India on the occurrence of cholera as an epidemic.

That the plan of encamping men, on such occasions, was in force so long ago as 1825,* we have distinct mention made in the official reports of that date. For example, in the report of the 31st Foot for that year, we learn that "previous to the 20th December, the regiment had suffered much from cholera while stationed in Fort William; but, on being encamped on the open plain or

* Report, 1826, page 111.

esplanade, the disease seemed immediately to abate, and ceased soon after."

In the Annual Report of the Inspector-General in Bengal for the years 1826 and 1827, we read as follows :—"On the 30th December (1826), they (the 13th, 38th, and 47th Regiments) reached Pahanagah, and were encamped in a low jungly position, with high grass; but on the night of the 31st December, cholera in its worst form broke out among them, and for four-and-twenty hours had a most alarming appearance, when it suddenly disappeared on the moving of the camp to a dry elevated situation, and clear of jungle ;" and two years afterwards we find Dr. Burke expressing himself in this way while writing on the effects of this measure,*—"The removal of the men to other quarters, or to tents, had in my experience here (Berhampore) and elsewhere, been of permanent benefit in choking or putting a stop to this disease, when"—he observes—"it was done in the proper and favourable season ; but," as he stated, "in the hot winds the encamping the men was found to be attended with no advantage, but the contrary, as was proved this year." Thus, the fact is rendered apparent that Dr. Burke, while well aware of the advantages of encamping troops on occasions of epidemics of this disease, was no less alive to the possible evils by which the measure might be attended if injudiciously carried out.

In 1835 the same measure was again put in force, and is thus recorded by the Inspector-General,†—"Several cases (of cholera) having occurred among the soldiers' wives (of the 49th Regiment in barracks) the surgeon was induced to recommend that half the families should be removed to a distant, though unfinished room, towards the end of the lines ;" and, it is added, "no case having occurred in the barracks after the removal, renders it more than probable that the atmosphere had lost its influence in that quarter." When, in 1842, cholera attacked the 29th Regi-

* Report for 1829, page 169.

† Report, 1835, page 322.

ment, the corps was stationed at Chinsurah. Between 22nd of August and 8th November, the disease carried off 50 men, besides women and children. On the latter date the Regiment began its march towards Ghazeepore, the sick, the women and childreu, proceeding by water ; and the circumstance was noted,* that immediately on the march being begun, the disease, which had so long clung to the men, appeared to cease. No further case occurred. Finally, when in August, 1843, the same disease attacked the 39th Regiment at Agra, the corps was moved into camp, at a distance of some five or six miles from cantonments. It there remained ten or twelve days, and with the best results, although the weather was most unfavourable, and the ground in a bad state on account of rain (Report, 1843).

It is due to the officers who, in 1833, administered the Government of India to mention in these pages the fact that they had become fully alive to the necessity of issuing, under authority, a brief code of instructions to be followed on occasions when the disease should make its appearance. A Board of Health, as it was, called or, in other words, a Sanitary Commission was accordingly appointed, the recommendations of which, as conveyed to the Inspector-General by the Secretary to Government,† are as follows, namely,—

"It was accordingly recommended that patients suffering from the disease be treated in a separate ward of the hospital, or in a distinct building.

"The bedding and bed-clothes that had been in use to be purified and fumigated ; those that cannot be so, to be destroyed.

"Bodies of men who die were to be interred with the least practicable delay, being conveyed to the graveyard in the covered cart for the purpose, and the body to be, if possible, exposed to aspersion by a solution of chloride, or to fumigation by one of the disinfecting gases.

---

* Report, 1842.

† In letter, dated 14th January, 1833.

" As perfect a segregation of the troops as possible was to be secured on occasions of their having to march through infected districts, or where the corps alone is infected, and the district not.

" When the disease has broken out extensively in barracks, and circumstances will permit, the corps should be marched out, and encamped in a dry, open, and elevated position."

Such, then, are some of the measures in former times adopted, with a view to combat this most terrible disease; measures which, in several respects, are identical with, and in all calculated to be quite as effectual for their purpose as those that have of late years been proposed with all the importance of novelties.